DESTINATION
INFINITY

DESTINATION INFINITY

*Reflections and Career Lessons
from a Road Warrior*

Jacquelyn Gaines

Arrie Publishing Company

Cary   New York   Atlanta   Miami

Destination Infinity-Reflections and Career Lessons from a Road Warrior.

Copyright © 2013 by Jacquelyn Gaines. All Rights Reserved. Printed in the United States of America. Published by Arrie Publishing Company, LLC. 201 Shannon Oaks Circle Suite 200, North Carolina 27511, USA.

Cover Design by Caprice+ Vision+ Media

Library of Congress Control Number: 2013956257

Library of Congress Cataloging-in-Publication Data
Gaines, Jacquelyn.
    Destination Infinity-Reflections and Career Lessons from a Road Warrior/Jacquelyn Gaines
    p. cm

ISBN-13: 978-0-9912285-0-8
ISBN-10: 0991228502

Printed in the United States of America

10 9 8 7 6 5 4 3 2 1

"The journey of a thousand miles begins with a single step."

~Lao Tzu

Table of Contents

DEDICATION

This book is dedicated to my dear husband, Wes, who had to tolerate so many of my travel challenges over the last two decades. Thanks for all the early morning drop-offs and late night pick-ups. Thanks for supporting me as I explored this other side of myself. I know it hasn't been easy and at times you probably wondered if you had a wife at all. Words will never be enough to express my gratitude. All I know is... I would not be at this place in my life without you.

Love, Jackie

PRELUDE

"You got to be careful if you don't know where you're going, because you might not get there."

~YOGI BERRA

It's 4am and I begin to drag my tired body from a restless night to get ready for the day ahead. Comfortable clothes, comfortable shoes and a suitcase precisely organized to give me maximum supplies for the week and just get in under the weight restrictions. Briefcase (a.k.a., traveling office) filled with all the tools of the trade and even some nuts and power bars to sustain me just in case I'm stranded. I glance over at my spouse, still fast asleep or mumbling "see you on Friday" and "have a safe trip."

I am part of a group of people called the Road Warriors...that army of professionals who travel as a significant part of our jobs. Whether by car, train or plane, we share a common bond. We can even spot other Road

Warriors along our journey. This has been my journey for the last five years. I could whine about the challenges of this life or share what most of us who do this kind of work have discovered—the treasure chest of knowledge and personal growth that being a Road Warrior can offer.

Using the experiences of Road Warriors, this book will offer reflections and career lessons found in that treasure chest. Many may give you pause about your own careers and some are parodies about life that will make you smile. Whatever your chosen profession, you will find a chapter that relates to your personal and professional journey. In the end you will see that there are no limits to where you can go if you leave that door open to the possibilities—destination infinity!

"To travel is to take a journey into yourself."

~**DANNY KAYE**

Keep Reading! This is not a travel book...but your passport to a successful career. Enjoy!

1

The Adventure Begins

"When preparing to travel, lay out all your clothes and all your money. Then take half the clothes and twice the money".

—UNKNOWN

Only three days left before my next travel day for work. How did my time at home go by so quickly? I had so many things I wanted to accomplish in my personal life, but I spent it making sure I was prepped for this next client visit on the West Coast. My office has all the documents neatly lined up that I will read on the plane so I have all the necessary facts on top of my mind. My spare bedroom serves as a staging room for the next two trips, because I know I won't have a lot of time to figure out outfits upon my return. I want and need maximum face time with my family and those I love in order to stay whole. This scenario is way too often the story of my life. I am constantly trying to find a state of balance between two worlds—home and the road. Success is totally related to my state of preparedness and state of mind.

Even when I enjoy the client I will be visiting or the location, I feel totally out of sorts when I don't fully prepare for the work ahead. When this happens, the time leading up to my departure is stressful affecting everyone around me. My "A" type personality does not allow me to experience this too often, but when it does, I can become overwhelmed and sometimes physically ill. That treasured family time is then compromised. You promise yourself and them that you will make up for it upon your return. Although, you know in your heart, as those words leave your lips, that you will be caught up in new madness, new trips to prepare for, as soon as your plane takes off for home. And the balancing act goes on. You pray for forgiveness, again.

As an Executive Health Care Consultant, I have to be "on" and "offer value" to the client with each interaction. Faking knowledge just doesn't cut it. You are also a solo act and cannot hide among the cast of characters in a less mobile organization. As a part of a team, you can take turns at "who's up first". So, if you have an off day, your colleagues can fill in the gaps. When all eyes are on **you**, there is no place to hide your inadequacies or shortcomings. You earn the role of trusted advisor to that client when you actually are equipped to advise. Advanced preparation is not an option. Faking a calm, self-assured, passionate demeanor is all dependent on the theatrical skills of the deliverer. You are definitely more genuine if you have that part of yourself together as well.

You don't have to be a Road Warrior to find the common threads to the life-cycle of your work days.

CAREER LESSONS LEARNED

Four key success factors to consider as you face a new work day:
- Advanced preparation
- Attention to work-life balance
- Adding value to your chosen profession
- Interactions that are genuine in words and actions

ADVANCED PREPARATION

Just like the Road Warrior thinks well in advance about all the things important to take and do before they will be disconnected from home base, we all have a variety of things that are important to us on any given day. What we choose to pay attention to is usually directly related to the level of urgency it holds for us.

This urgency could be: 1) crisis oriented (real or perceived), 2) time sensitive issues, 3) pressure from leadership, customers or family, or 4) where your interests or passions lie. For highly organized individuals, **their goal is to minimize the urgency factor by constantly looking ahead and course correcting as needed.** This way, if a crisis does occur needing your immediate attention; it does not take plans for the day completely off course. Bosses are generally happier because your response and actions are timelier and it allows more time to explore the things that fuel your passion. If you are a leader in the organization, this is the difference between proactive and reactive leadership. Which one wears you out mentally and physically? Which one takes your stress level to a different place and leads to relationship challenges all around you? Reactive work is never a good thing if you have choices to influence a different ending.

Not everyone is highly organized from birth. We may have some predisposition or learned behaviors from our parents, but for the most part, it takes skill, will and practice. Here are some tips that may help those who are still developing their organizational skill set:

- **Journal the important things**- dates, projects, family milestones. In the midst of the craziness of our lives, we all need gentle reminders of what's in front of us. In leadership you are constantly (sometimes several times a day) reshuffling that deck of important things. Journaling can also help you think through complex issues. Seeing things in print helps our mind naturally put things in a clearer perspective than when the thoughts are just bouncing around in our head.
- **Use technology to prompt you.** With so many gadgets on the market today that are inextricably tied to our hips, purses and laps,

we should have enough opportunities for one of these toys to buzz, sing or ring us into awareness of what's ahead so we can be better prepared.

- **Include others in prioritizing your work**. Almost every time I am with a client, I hear the words... "My plate is so full" or "I am overwhelmed". Here's a reality check- the plate will always be full so get over it. The trick is to learn how to manage what is there, knowing that something else will always be added. Share your plate with others. Talk about how you can accomplish shared goals or projects more effectively. Two brains working together are always better than going it alone. Proactively re-prioritize with your boss to make sure you are focused on what's really important. (Hint: this works pretty well with loved ones too!)

- **Don't procrastinate!** We may think we are giving ourselves more breathing room, when actually we are creating more stress and chaos when we procrastinate. In the workplace, this can lead to errors, miscommunication and a less than desirable outcome.

- **Do your homework on the issues.** Advanced preparation means gathering all that you need to be at the top of your game. Today there is so much access to information that we don't have to go far. The depth of the internet (at least the reliable sources) can offer background on a client or a recipe for Aunt Sue at the family reunion. If someone is counting on you to be the expert- know something before you are face to face with them.

Attention to Work-Life Balance

Everyday we are faced with a series of choices. In a typical 9am-5pm workday, how you use those designated hours has pretty much been decided for you—**work** is on the agenda. For the Road Warrior, those hours dedicated to work are not so clear and often cross over into the time that most who are in today's workforce can draw a line in the sand and say, "I am clocked out for the day and going home." Most can turn off their business phones and unplug from their work-life and plug into their home life. Now, it may take a little time during this daily transition to decompress and shake off all the challenges of the day, but the line (based on time alone) is clear.

Road Warriors have to proactively draw their own lines. Travel days often begin on a Sunday and end when your plane touches back down in that state called home. Preparation for both travel and the client on the other end can even dip into sacred Saturdays most count on for renewal and recharging with family and friends. It's the time, if we haven't worked out all week, we run, or hit the gym. Even evenings or nights can have work creep, as you catch up on reports or are constantly checking your phone for messages you don't want to be overwhelmed by in the morning. So, where is the proverbial work-life balance? How do you nurture personal relationships and find the time to take care of yourself- mind, body, and spirit?

The wrong answer is to do nothing and accept this crazy hand that you have chosen for yourself. Or, you can take back your life and get a game plan that values the flip side to your work life. Pay attention to finding balance. The alternative can lead to divorce, stress, depression and physical illness. These are just a few examples that are at the top the list of potential unhealthy outcomes.

As our world becomes more high tech, with gadgets that follow us everywhere, the lines between work and home get more blurred every day. So, even in a 9am- 5pm job, where the clock officially dictates your "on and off time", the advances in technology contributes to the ability to stay "connected" to work. No longer is this just the purview of a Road Warrior.

Tips to Finding Balance:

- **Reconcile with yourself that having a balanced life is important.** Sometimes, we get so caught up in the desire to have all the nice things that life has to offer (i.e., cars, houses, wealth, prestige), that we push our work side to the edge trying to get there. The easiest thing to place second in our lives is attention to ourselves and those around us. Yet, making decisions that place you second, can have the most devastating and long-term impact on the quality of your life. You have to make a conscious effort to balance that scale. For some, it can be a daily challenge. However, commitment and due diligence to your well-being is critical.

- **Quality Time can help to counterbalance Quantity of Time.** No matter how many designated hours your work day includes, the time you are "at home"- be "at home." Unplug from all the gadgets, focus on those you love, engage in conversations that have nothing to do with work, exercise or just meditate to clear you mind. Whatever you choose to do, focus on you. Any challenges you have at work will be better dealt with the next day if you have had a chance to recharge and renew. For those addicted to technology, this will definitely take time (and maybe therapy-smile) to feel comfortable with disconnecting. Put your toys out of sight and sound. In a true emergency, the land line still works as a method of communication.

- **Calendar timeout's.** Proactively calendar timeouts or dates with yourself. Hold them as sacred as your other appointments. Start small with 30 minutes a day (at a minimum) and work your way up to larger blocks of time. Tell others that this is sacred personal time that cannot be touched. And try not to make a laundry list of excuses to fill that time with more work. There will always be times when this becomes a necessity, but those times should be the exception and not the rule. For those who are Road Warriors, this is doable. It just requires as much thought as getting ready for that next trip.

ADDING VALUE TO YOUR CHOSEN PROFESSION

The assignments of a Road Warrior are usually connected to a contract with a certain expected deliverable or result attached to it. In order to get paid or continue to work for that client, you must meet and hopefully exceed expectations. The best fit between the client and Road Warrior is when their values match and when the work is grounded in a shared passion for success...each part contributing to something bigger than the needs of just one. When there is no passion to participate in that work, only the need to go through the motions to get through the day, the results never reach their maximum potential. In other words, we fake knowledge and sometimes skills; we watch the clock and our work relationships are weak. Our motivation is to stay under the radar to get a check.

Economic viability is always an important life consideration. However, if that's your driving motivation for the work you do, you are one miserable employee. Most employees want to feel as if their contribution adds value. However, just showing up to work does not get you that outcome. Work cannot be a passive interaction. One must engage, proactively gain the knowledge and skills needed to be at the top of your game and execute effectively and efficiently.

An underlying foundation for the company I currently work for (The Studer Group, Inc.) is "purposeful worthwhile work and making a difference." We should all seek careers that give us the opportunity to contribute to something bigger than ourselves.

Tips to Adding Value to Your Profession

- **Figure out the work that brings you joy.** Sometimes life and the need for economic survival force us to make career or job choices that may not match our passion. That doesn't mean you should not continue to seek the knowledge and skills to get you where you want to be. And, it does not mean you cannot engage in your current work because it is not an exact match. Find one thing you feel good about that can continue to motivate you to do more than just get by. When we spend so much of our life at work, just getting by is a terrible existence.

- **Remember, you are being paid for a deliverable.** All employers expect a result from employees in exchange for that paycheck. They hired you for the value that you bring. You don't need a Road Warrior contract for that to be spelled out to you. Just check out your job descriptions. The deliverables are outlined there.

- **Proactively seek out career development opportunities.** Don't wait for your future to be handed to you. Take a class, find a mentor or read a book. The growth you achieve will most definitely add value to your place of employment. However, the ultimate winner is the value it adds to you.

INTERACTIONS ARE GENUINE IN WORDS AND ACTIONS

Road Warriors arrive at their designated locations and often have limited time to make a good impression and get to pushing toward the expected deliverables of the contract. They are expected to come with a toolbox full of tools and tactics to take an organization to a higher level of performance. The one thing that is difficult to mask under the nice suits and opening smiles is if the Road Warrior is disingenuous. Many organizations have asked for consultants to be replaced because they never quite fit as a trusted advisor. Trust being the operative word in that equation. At the heart of this outcome is the lack of an emotional connection that says you are someone they can believe in.

The only difference with those in less mobile jobs is the time allowed to develop relationships. Interactions are almost daily and you often get a peek at the personal lives of your colleagues. The more we know about one another, the richer the relationships. Trust and reliability is built over time. For those in leadership roles, the same pressure exists for immediate acceptance. The magnifying glass is directly aimed at everything –words and actions. Being genuine is an important ingredient for success.

Tips for a Genuine You!

- **Be comfortable in your own skin.** This comes with having the knowledge and skills to face the task ahead of you. Don't fake knowledge. Your shortcomings will eventually come to the surface and destroy any early trust achieved. Seek others that may be able to assist you. No one knows it all.

- **Practice respectful truth-telling.** Even if employees do not like you, they may still find you a credible person if you are always respectful and tell the truth. Unpleasant information may not be what we want to hear, but if it is delivered in a respectful manner, it is easier to digest. Tone of voice, body language and the words we choose to use all make a difference. If your emotions are running high, take a break until you have control of yourself and your presentation to others.

- **Stay true to your promises.** If you have made promises related to expectations, always keep the communication channels open while relating progress along the way. If it looks like you will fall short, explain why and revise the expectations with the other person. Lack of timely follow-up can be destructive to your path to a genuine you. Remember, being genuine is both a perception held by others of you and how you perceive yourself at your core.

"My fear of flying starts as soon as I buckle myself in and then the guy up front mumbles a few unintelligible words then before I know it I'm thrust into the back of my seat by acceleration that seems way too fast and the rest of the trip is an endless nightmare of turbulence, of near misses. And then the cabbie drops me off at the airport."

DENNIS MILLER, TALK SHOW HOST

2

What's in Your Luggage?

"Own only what you can always carry with you: know languages, know countries, know people. Let your memory be your travel bag."

—ALEKSANDR SOLZHENITSYN

Choices, choices, choices. Before every trip I am faced with a series of decisions. What clothes do I need to take to match the climate and the organizational culture at the end of my destination? Large suitcase or mid-size will depend on how long I will be gone this time. All my choices are bound by one common denominator- the 50 pound weight limit per bag.

I use my hands to estimate the weight of each piece as I carefully place my clothes for the week in the chosen bag. Since I have taken this Road Warrior job, my entire shopping has changed to look for lightweight clothes that look nice and don't wrinkle. (I don't think I have bought linen clothing in years.) I have separate toiletry bags for each piece of luggage-cutting down on the time to repack for the next trip. I include healthy snacks, fruit and oatmeal just in case. And, with one final weigh-in using the bathroom scale, I am good to go.

Isn't it fascinating the amount of time we will spend attending to the details of things like clothing and travel supplies? We even get upset with ourselves when we forget an item we thought we really needed to make us feel complete. Yet the most important things we really need are not found inside our luggage, but inside ourselves. It's our attitudes, our beliefs and biases attached. It's our demeanor that can overshadow any piece of clothing we may wear. **How often, with the same methodical approach do we evaluate our end destination and what we need to "unpack" or adjust as we enter a new environment? The weight limits in this case are all the cultural and organizational norms we may need to adhere to upon arrival.** My guess is this is an area most of us don't spend much time on at all.

There are stark parallels between preparation for travel and how we prepare for work each day. We methodically choose our clothes, our shoes and maybe even pack ourselves a lunch. The "weight limits" in this case are the dress codes and norms of that organization.Our choices will influence acceptance or whether we are the water cooler topic of conversation. If our choices are too extreme, it may even land us with a written warning about a breech in one of the organizational codes of conduct.

And, we have to pay attention when we are hired to know these basic norms. Casual Fridays are taking over many businesses today, even allowing jeans that were never a part of any organizational norm ten years ago. Casual shirts with no ties for men and no hose for women are becoming the norm. (Just for the record, I am not complaining about the hose...long overdue!) Look at companies like *Apple* - I am not sure suits were ever a part of their work culture.

The multi-generations in the workplace today could account for the changes we see in organizational norms. For us fifty and beyond, acclimating to the new rules can be difficult, even uncomfortable. Professional demeanor was that suit and anything different meant you did not want to be taken seriously or respected in your role. For those in their twenty's or thirty's, wearing a suit to work may be a deal breaker for employment-for them. I think both generations would agree to some of the extreme behaviors that breech the code of conduct at work- like micro-mini dresses or skirts, too much exposure of body parts or being generally unclean. We absolutely live in rapidly changing, interesting times. Who knows where the pendulum may swing in ten more years? Suits at work may make a comeback. I sure hope the acceptance of micro-mini's or exposed body parts happens after my retirement! Enough said.

Paying attention to those *other* cues, like attitudes and unwritten cultural norms, is often left "packed" inside ourselves. We fail to research those other elements that may affect our engagement and job satisfaction. In other words, we do not take enough time to figure out organizational culture before we say "yes" to accepting employment. We think we can make it work or "fit in" no matter what. This is especially true if our economic needs are driving us to that job...any job. By default, we are forced to make internal adjustments to survive. And, now we are in a 9 am- to- 5 pm job we don't like. Our performance is marginal and it's a miserable way to spend most of your waking hours.

Here's a page from my own career journal:

After living on the West Coast for almost eight years, I began to get homesick for my family and children living on the East Coast. Distance and job responsibilities only made it possible to be together with them two to three times a year. I felt an internal tug to move back home. I am not sure which part of me was pulling me more-the need to be closer to family or the fact that I didn't have many upwardly mobile options available to me in my current job. I was at the top of my game. I didn't dislike the work or the people, I just wanted something more. The eight hour trek across country to close that familial gap was also a significant variable. I didn't actively search for another job on the east coast, but I think once your mind and heart get to this place together, you begin to hear possibilities you filtered out in the past.

So, against my husband's intuition, I accepted a position as the Regional President of a multi-hospital health system in Pennsylvania. Definitely a major step in my career and got me only driving distance away from those I love. I really believe my internal radar about people and culture must have been completely turned off. I am usually so good at sensing these things pretty quickly. It is what gives me an edge in the work that I do. In this case, I believe my desire to relocate "home" and advance, overshadowed my common sense. I never picked up on the organizational and cultural cues that my family and I would face upon arrival.

This part of Pennsylvania was cold- literally and figuratively. Old coal mining country we were told. On a regular basis the temperature would dip to 10 degrees or lower in the winter and would drop 18 inches of the heaviest snow I ever shoveled. What was I thinking? I hate cold weather and shoveling doesn't ring my bell either. We probably could have acclimated to the cold, but the people were a whole other story. Some had a palpable "coldness" toward each other that I had never really experienced before on such a large scale. Such sadness reflected deep in their eyes. You really wanted to put Prozac in the public drinking water to see if it would make a difference. How on earth did I miss that when the Board of Directors interviewed me? How did I miss that when we came back to look for a house? Why didn't I pick up on the racism and sexism present at this community's core? Unfortunately, after accepting the job, I experienced both. I discuss more of this in my book, "Believing You Can Fly." When I packed for these trips I think I left my common sense and internal radar at home. My husband's radar, however, was in over-drive. He tried to warn me, but didn't want to be unsupportive of something I thought would make me happy.

It took less than a month before my common sense returned and my internal radar re-engaged. The reality of the mistake I had made in choosing to live and work in an organization and community that was so completely opposite to my personal values and beliefs was overwhelming. I gave it a good run for almost three years before we could move out of this miserable place. What a toll it took on my personal life. Yes, I made it to a career that many minority professionals never achieve, but at what cost.

I often wonder where I would be today, if I had not been blinded by that internal tug to relocate and advance. I just wish I had done my homework on the community and got to know the organizational culture a little bit deeper. I could have called others familiar with the organization and area. I could have looked at the retention rate of past executives working for that organization. If I had, I would have discovered the higher than normal turn-over rate. I would have been told about the underlying sadness or prevalence of depression in a community that seems to have been trapped in a time capsule from 40-50 years ago. And, I know three years of my life and that of my family would not have been compromised waking up each day wishing we were somewhere else.

Career Lessons Learned

- Be deliberate in researching organizational and cultural norms of the places you would like to work- before hire.
- Don't leave your common sense and intuition at home when interviewing. It's better to over-analyze cultural fit rather than make a bad decision affecting your future.
- After hire, stay alert to shifts in culture. If the compromise required for alignment to the new culture will dramatically affect your personal integrity or well-being...start shopping for a new job.

TIPS TO PACKING WHAT YOU REALLY NEED!

Deliberate Research

When trying to gain knowledge about a potential employer, there are many options available to you. Today, most organizations have web pages that can give you a general overview of the values, structure, financial status and even names of the Board of Directors and Executive Leadership. Remember, these web pages are intended to present the organization in a positive light. So, any underlying issues or unwritten cultural norms will not be found there. However, you may be amazed at what you find if you research the local newspapers and public records, putting in the organizational name in the search engine. Newspapers love to dish dirt and if there was some to be found, it may raise its ugly head in the local rag. You can do the same with Executive Leadership and Board Members. Google them and see what you find. I was actually shocked to see what was even under my name when I Googled myself- unauthorized stuff spanning my career that I didn't even know was open for public consumption.

Don't stop there! Find people who know anything about the inside of the organization and ask for their honest assessment of culture. Ask them,

"What is important for me to know about organizational culture that could impact my success?"

"What impresses you about this organization and what concerns you?"

"How would you describe the leadership style of the Executive Team?" (This one is important because they set overall cultural tone.)

"Are there unwritten rules I should be aware of- sacred cows?"

"What is considered acceptable and unacceptable behavior?"

"Would you call this a fair organization?"

"Do you like working for this company?" (If they are a current employee)

"What made you leave?" (If a past employee)

"Would you recommend this organization as a great place to work?" If the answer is yes, "Can you tell me why?"

Don't stop there! When visiting the new community you may live, go to the grocery stores, local shopping centers and restaurants. Check out the churches if that's important to you as well. Don't just observe when you are there...talk to the locals. Without letting on that you are researching for a job, ask questions about the potential place of employment. "I am new to the area and noticed that beautiful hospital down the street. Is it a great place to get care?" It usually doesn't take much for a potential neighbor to share their opinions, both positive and negative. If they are really passionate about it, you could be standing there for quite a while getting an earful.

Now, it doesn't mean that everything people tell you or what you may find after a good *Google* search is 100% true. However, you are searching for common threads and a peek at organizational and community culture. Write down what excites you, questions unanswered and things that give you that funny feeling in the pit of your stomach that this may not be the right fit. Proactively ask clarifying questions during the interview, probably surprising the potential employer that you did any research at all. These same tips can be applied to a change of employment in your existing community. No two organizational cultures are exactly alike. Make sure you can live with the rules of the road.

Pack Your Common Sense and Intuition

After my experience in Pennsylvania, I know I will never analyze a new job opportunity the same way again. I am so hyper-vigilant about getting as much information as I can to make the best decisions possible about my career. I also try to be more open to those who know me best about cultural fit. Sometimes we all can be blinded by any number of variables important to us personally and professionally. We need those human mirrors that we trust to reflect when our common sense and intuition did not make the trip. Consider the impact on all members of your family who are on the journey with you. Fit is just as important to their happiness as well. Bad choices affect everyone.

Stay Alert to Cultural Shifts- Assess, Align or Leave

Mergers, acquisitions and constant change in leadership are prevalent throughout the business world. Some are driven by greed, many because of our strained economy. With every change is the potential for a change in organizational culture. One leader may have a more "team spirited" leadership style. Another may be completely autocratic in nature. Mergers and acquisitions can be even more disruptive as two whole organizational cultures must decide whose house rules stand.

I once worked for a newly hired CEO who stated publicly that calling him by anything other than Mr. (last name) was totally unacceptable under any circumstances. This was a complete 180 degrees from the stance of the prior CEO who welcomed first name relationships. His denigrating style began to erode the very values that organization had been built upon. He began to replace people in significant leadership roles with those leaders he knew would support his humungous ego. (I guess you can tell this change did not sit with me too well.)It's times like this you have to have a good long talk with yourself and decide if this is still the right fit and the organizational culture you can support going forward.

- Take the time to assess the extent of change you are willing to tolerate.
- Reconcile the compromise you will need to make and align if you choose to stay.

If the compromise is too great (personally and professionally)-actively choose to leave. Even if you choose to stay and don't get with the program...sometimes the end result is the same. Except, this time it would not be **your** choice to leave.

- Never compromise your integrity for anyone or any organization. Find other options.

3

Lines and a Pat Down- Oh Joy!

"When traveling with someone, take large doses of patience and tolerance with your morning coffee".

— HELEN HAYES

The line ahead of you moves at a snail's pace as each person ahead of you gets ready for their upcoming debut. You can see the anxiety on the faces of some as it gets closer to their turn. Some chat about their need to go through the required ritual, while others chat about how ridiculous the whole experience is. Whatever is their opinion of the experience, they all go through the steps with one shared mission- to get to the other side.

Lights, cameras (literally), action... and the "security striptease begins." Shoes, coats, belts, and scarves all neatly in the bin and we proceed to shuffle with trepidation through metal detectors and x-ray machines. Hands up, legs apart...you can almost hear the accompanying music. You may even try to teleport yourself to another place mentally to minimize the personal trauma. Then the security personnel bring you down to earth with a cold, "you are done." Or, "we need to pat you down." If the latter is your prize, you now feel the groping and probing of a complete stranger; no different than if you were that dancer in a strip joint minus the money in your waistband. Then the music stops and off you go to replace all clothing removed, readjust to the experience and proceed to find your gate. Good grief! The things we endure when we have to.

For the Road Warrior, this is our weekly ritual. Don't think for one minute that just because we travel often, the emotions tied with getting through airport security aren't still alive and impactful. But, we all do it. These repeated mental and emotional readjustments are requirements for the job. We strip and shuffle. We stand there exposing our vulnerabilities as our personal belongings move along the conveyor belt. They may be groped and probed as well. We endure because we like getting a paycheck for the work we do. We can't get that check if we don't do the dance. Sound familiar?

Career Lessons Learned

- All work will require ongoing mental and emotional readjustments every day. Your ability to comply is directly influenced by the magnitude of the readjustment, past experiences, rewards and recognition and the perceived risk of "non-compliance."
- Know the organizational "rules." This includes standards of behavior or codes of conduct- written and unwritten. Knowledge is a powerful antidote for the unknown and fear-based emotions.

SURVIVAL TIPS FOR YOUR NEXT STRIPTEASE!

Following the rules at work actually begins prior to hire. You may remember getting a contract of employment which included an attachment called "standards of behavior" or "codes of conduct." Once we get past the salary and benefits, we skim through the rest of the documents which could give us additional clues about organizational culture and expectations of employment. These rules can include the usual suspects like attendance, smoking and dress codes, and the not so explicit- respect, courtesy and teamwork. Most are harmless on the surface, unless they are in conflict with your own points of view.

Imagine a job where uniforms were required. If the standard issue was not complimentary to your body type, putting that uniform on everyday makes you vulnerable to all your co-workers. Even ordering the uniform with other new hires can be embarrassing if you must order a larger size to make it work. Can you imagine the stress of a model, actress or even the First Lady? Throughout their entire careers they are under the microscope for any change in appearance or demeanor. To achieve and sustain success, weight loss by any means necessary is often an imperative to acceptance. And, they do it! The need for fame and fortune exceeds their common sense about the real impact on their health. Pictures of anorexic young women in Hollywood on the red carpet, with gowns literally hanging off their bodies, demonstrate their compliance to the "rules". Non-compliance could mean they don't get picked up for the next job. For the First Lady, the country's obsession with her muscular arms is over the top. How many hours do you think she now works out to keep that positive image alive? Muscular arms are now the unwritten rule. (It's a good thing I am not the First Lady. I would have a big hill to climb for that rule.)

> Know the rules and know yourself! Take the time to read the fine print of the employment contract, including codes of conduct. How far are you willing to go? And, know the result of non-compliance.

I remember being hired for a job where image was so important, that they hired an image consultant to offer an assessment of our "current state" upon hire and to offer recommendations for improvement. I had been in significant professional jobs for more than 30 years. Being from the baby boomer generation meant suits were the norm in the workplace. So, needless to say, compared to the younger female new hires, with their low cut blouses and up-cut skirts, I felt I was in good shape to pass the inspection. I actually was somewhat insulted at having to endure this consult, but tried to stay focused on the fact that it was one of the rules of employment. At my age I was trying to cover up flaws, not having a strange man looking for them. My anxiety was through the roof. I couldn't even sleep the night before thinking about this unwelcome encounter. Maybe I would walk away with something to improve.

The next day, a very flamboyant young man, at least 20 years younger than me, entered the room and immediately came over and whisked the chair I was in over to the large mirror against the wall. "Hello" was lost the moment he began shaking my sharply styled hair. He started by saying I had nice hair but it was too flat and needed to be teased and fluffed. This was definitely his first mistake. I guess no one gave him the memo that you never touch a black woman's hair! Seeing the look on my face, he stopped and went on to ask me to stand. Because of my height, he encouraged me to wear high waist pants. It took everything in me not to laugh out loud. That recommendation would never happen. All his recommendations matched his generation or some warped fashion sense. It didn't seem that it was about professionalism at all. I said thanks and left with angst about the organization I had just joined. Would I really have to comply with these "rules" or maintain the professional demeanor that has worked for me for decades? Not sure.

That image consult left a bad taste in my mouth, so I set up a time to discuss my concerns with my new boss. I clarified the rules for appearance and confirmed that I was just fine. I was told that the company started doing these consults as a way to help younger hires that had yet to draw the line between "work" and "play" clothes. Another important career lesson learned- **Ask for clarity. If you don't understand the rules, don't assume their intent or the result of non-compliance. Then decide if you can live within those rules.**

A bonus from this experience was that the company realized they needed to take a different approach...one size did not fit all.

4

Did You Really Wear That?

"Be careless in your dress if you will, but keep a tidy soul."

— MARK TWAIN

Pink hair, green hair, blue and yellow makes four
　　Long skirts, short skirts, no skirts...more...

Probably sounds like the beginning of a nursery rhyme or a passage from a Dr. Seuss book. Actually, they are the real sights that a Road Warrior may see on any given day just sitting in an airport! Sometimes I find myself literally trying not to laugh aloud or feeling a tug at my heart because the view makes me sad. I have witnessed the sheer joy of a family going on, what appeared to be, their first vacation to a far off destination. I have seen abuse (verbal and physical) and, the other extreme that was abuse for my eyes- a little too much PDA (public display of affection). That story got weirder as this young couple aggressively making out in the terminal waiting area was joined by the young woman's parents. They said nothing and the two continued their show. The young woman looked to be about 16 years old. The young man was not much older. I can tell you, if these were my kids, the script for this show would have dramatically changed upon my arrival and one of those two young people may have been going home. And in another era, my father would have been laying hands—and not in a spiritual way.

If you are really bored, your mind starts to wander and your creative energy steps in and all of a sudden you have created whole stories about the lives of the people around you. Sometimes, bits and pieces of conversations you overhear add additional character to the story in your mind. You may even go so far to convince yourself, you have it all figured out before you board.

Your stories are colored by past experiences, cultural biases and a whole boat load of variables we have stored inside (hearts and minds) over the course of a lifetime. Isn't it amazing how quick we size people up without any knowledge at all except external presentation? *People watching* is often a past-time of the Road Warrior, especially on those long layovers or delays. It occurred to me one day how these quick assumptions are so similar to how we "size people up" in the workplace. I would probably not be wrong to go further to say- we even have created our own mental image of the lives of our co-workers, based on nothing but external presentation or what may be rolling around our heads.

Career Lesson Learned

- Beware of first impressions –they directly impact relationships and decision-making in the workplace.
- Validate your assumptions...better yet, ask before you assume.

Without conversation and relationships that go further than just the surface, our assumptions and self-made stories can color our interactions. What do we really know without validation? The answer is- not much. I am sure many of you have been shocked to learn you have been totally wrong about another individual you "sized-up". If their first impression was not so great or you were so distracted by their external presentation, all future interactions were tainted by the story you created about them in your head. When you finally were *able to hear* a different story, you may have even been embarrassed by your first assumption.

I deliberately said "able to hear" because often, we can be so entrenched in our beliefs and assumptions that it blocks our ability to really "listen" for an alternative story. Not convinced or you don't think this happens to you? Let's try a simple exercise.

> You are now the CEO of an organization and have an opening for a new leader to run one of your major departments. Based on only the descriptions below, which would you select as the best candidate? No other information is available. What's your first thought when you read the description (first impression)? Don't pick politically correct, stay with what "you" really think. What mental pictures come to mind?
>
> - A morbidly obese female with her graduate degree
> - A homeless man recently separated from his wife and three children
> - A white male with his bachelor's degree
> - A single Latino female with one child
> - An Asian man running his own nail salon business

So, who did you choose? If you are really honest with yourself, you all felt a tug in your gut at this uncomfortable exercise which hooks a variety of cultural stereotypes we try to tell ourselves are not inside our minds. No matter how much education we may have, we have been programmed our entire life to these filters which can subconsciously affect our professional and personal judgment and relationships. How quick did you get to a mental image with just words? Don't be surprised. These mental images have been set and reset by our parents, our friends, past experiences (even if only one time), and definitely by the media. We would be dishonest to try and discount them and say..."I don't have a problem in this area". We all do in some form or fashion.

For example, homelessness is often equated with dirty clothes, substance abuse, mental illness and living on the streets. How does that image change when your daughter or son cannot afford their apartment anymore and you allow them to move back into *your home*? Are they not *homeless?* The former image applied to one of your children would mortify you... same result...different story.

The real challenge for each of us is our ability to reconcile our assumptions *before* we pass judgment that is often difficult to reverse. People watching and daydreaming about the stories of those we may never see again is harmless. However, in the workplace, the ramifications of unsubstantiated stories can be disruptive (even destructive)to relationships and achieving organizational outcomes.

TIPS FOR EFFECTIVE VALIDATION AND USE OF STORIES

Check yourself in the mirror and be honest about the reflection looking back at you.

What biases color your lens about others personally and professionally? Be open to getting feedback from others about how you may be responding to others. This first step is courageous and requires a degree of humbleness to "seek what you don't know" about yourself.

Validate your gut!

Even the most intuitive person cannot be sure about their conclusions about others unless they ask clarifying questions. External presentations and perceived behavior only tell you part of the story (maybe). Engage in conversations first hand if you really want that other person's "truth". Ask open ended questions that allow them to share and not closed questions that lead with your assumptions. For those in leadership roles, this is a constant challenge to watch the words used with the workforce.

- For example, "Tell me a little bit about yourself and your passion?" is a very different question than, "Whoa, you look like you have had quite a rough career journey, right?" Which question would you prefer to answer? Which question hooks you emotionally or says, "I really want to get to know you." The latter says your mind had already reached a conclusion.

- How about a more sensitive assumption? "Are you sure you can handle being a single Mom and the responsibilities of this job?" or "Are there any challenges that may prevent you from being able to step into this new role?" The first question lets the employee know you already have thoughts about single moms. The latter, still shows concern, yet offers the employee the opportunity to share their perception of possible constraints. All single moms do not have the same work challenges if any. In this era of extended families living together, it may not be an issue at all if Grandma is the caretaker. They actually may have more support than a two-working parent household!

- Beware of second and third hand interpretation. Talk directly to the person you are seeking clarifying information. The further away from the source, you are now allowing other's "guts" or assumptions to color the story. Haven't you ever played the childhood game of "**Telephone**"? That's when you sit in a circle and whisper in the ear a phrase and pass it on around the circle to see if the message is the same once all members in the circle have passed it on. Usually, it is NEVER the same. Sometimes, completely unrecognizable to the person starting the game. Each person will add their twist to the phrase or change it all together. The basic premise of this game is no different than communication patterns in the workplace. We always add our twist to the story. So, the only real "truth" is directly from the horse's mouth. Even though it is so much easier and more comfortable to ask others. I am not sure the fear of direct communication, except maybe it won't validate our assumptions.

Non-verbal communication speaks louder than words.

Just when you think you have your assumptions and biases under control, those dang non-verbal's leap from your face and posture. Everything you carefully etched in your mind to say was totally overshadowed by that face telling a different story. Sometimes we may not even be aware that we have "the look".

We all have experienced "the look" from another individual. Didn't you absolutely know when your parents meant "I am not playing, get it together!" My father didn't have to speak...a stern look across the dinner table meant I had crossed the line and for me to be quiet or I may have trouble sitting down real soon. Now, don't go call the parent police! I am from a different era when spanking was the norm.

As an Executive, I have been told that I get "the look", when I am passionate and am really not open for a second opinion. (I never knew this until one of my senior leaders had the courage to bring it to my attention.) As a consultant, I am hyper-vigilant about my words matching my non-verbal expressions. It is important to give honest messages to the people I work with and not leave them wondering what I *really* think or feel about them. This is imperative when your interactions with them are so limited. No time to build the depth of relationships afforded in a 9am-5pm job. In my personal life, I use "the look" to my advantage. Not with everything, but not a bad tool for when my grandsons are trying to act up at a crowded restaurant. I can feel myself channeling my father. Even at a young age, these boys received my message.

Discover the power of proactive story-telling.

Many cultures often express themselves in storytelling. It is through stories of our life's journey that we offer a window to our soul. Each of our stories, as are our lives, is unique. For the listener, it can be difficult sometimes to relate to another's journey...especially the part that may reflect pain or sorrow. You may even wonder why it is important for you to hear since it is not something real for you. To really grow personally and professionally...it is important to listen, even solicit stories that may differ from your own. Even though they may make you uncomfortable...it may help you walk in another's shoes for just a moment and "understand" a little bit more. As a leader it is a powerful connector between you and your staff. Take the opportunity to get below the surface with others you spend so many of your waking hours with. Go for a cup of coffee together, take a walk during break or just show genuine interest when others share on their own. Leaders can even have story-telling integrated as a part of team meetings. For example, they could have each person in the meeting take turns telling one thing they think no one would know about them. This can be fun and team building.

None of this means an individual has to share all the intimacies of their personal life. It means allowing others to share what is important to them. Story-telling offers an opportunity to dismantle those tightly held biases embedded in each of us. Some may actually walk away with a change in base assumptions. Proactive story-telling *will* impact future and existing relationships in the workplace. Give it a try.There is nothing to lose and so much to gain.

"The emperor is naked!

"The parade stopped. The emperor paused. A hush fell over the crowd, until one quick-thinking peasant shouted:"

No, he isn't. The emperor is merely endorsing a clothing-optional lifestyle!"

JAMES FINN GARNER

5

Death by Hamburger

"You can find your way across this country using burger joints the way a navigator uses stars."

CHARLES KURALT

7:45 pm. Finally, the plane arrives at the connecting airport for the next flight. The Road Warrior knows she/he have exactly one hour to get to the next gate, hit the restroom and find sustenance. First, they take care of the bio-essentials, then food. Imaginary spear in hand, the hunt begins. Tonight, this carnivore needs meat. No wilted salads, no yogurt, no fruit in a cup...M-E-A-T. And like a tiger looking for prey, all senses are in high gear. The smells of a variety of choices fill the road ahead with hot dogs, pepperoni pizza and hamburgers, hamburgers, hamburgers.... Sadly, the pre-made sandwiches lost their smell the day before and do not draw the interest of the hungry Road Warrior. As the Road Warrior gets closer to the departure gate, a decision must be made. There is no time to spare. All seem evil (and definitely border on unhealthy territory). When all the choices are bad...what's a Road Warrior to do?

"Cheeseburger please, but hold the fries. I had enough carbs on the plane with the array of pretzels and biscotti." The sign at McDonald's says a cheeseburger has 330 calories. Add in the biscotti at 200 calories and the pretzels at 60 calories...dinner was a whopping 590 calories. Not the best choice, but better than that fried chicken basket at 1,200 calories.

So how in the world does this relate to your career? Periodically, in our work lives, we are all faced with times when none of the options in front of us are what we really want. We are forced to make a decision out of an assortment of less than optimal options. This could range from the career choice itself or small task oriented decisions specific to a project you are working on. For example, economic survival often forces people to take on jobs just to make ends meet. They may not like the choice, but it may offer a salary to sustain them until they are able to get what they want. Some may even take a lesser job in title and pay as a way to get them a "foot in the door" to a better position in a company they have longed to work for. We have all heard of people who have literally worked themselves up from the bottom and are now leaders in organizations.

Sometimes, learning the company work by actually starting at a lower position can offer you deeper insights you would seldom receive if you just started at the top. The current TV show- **Undercover Boss**- is a good example of lessons learned when these very powerful CEO's took on the roles of their employees. Revelations about what actually happens in their operationscome to light in every episode, giving them new insights about changes they may need to make or recognition of employees doing ex-traordinary things.

Throughout my career, I have done everything from the bedside(as a registered nurse) to the Board room (as a Regional President and CEO of a health system). In each role, I learned a bit more about myself and I am convinced, each of those experiences contributed to me being a better leader. If nothing else, it surely gave me material for my books for years to come.I am not sure I consciously chose lesser positions to get ahead, but left myself open to the possibility of "trying on different shoes" not exactly knowing where it would lead. Sometimes, the money was less than desirable and the environment or culture a little scary...but it was the best fit for me at the time in my career journey.

CAREER LESSON LEARNED

- During our career lifetime, we all will face times when the choices ahead of us seem less than optimal. Weigh the risk and the benefit of each choice, then move forward. Put more personal energy into appreciating the benefits of that choice than dwelling on the lack of a perfect fit...at least until you are able to find a more optimal choice.
- If you always wait for the perfect choice, you may deprive yourself of needed essentials.
- Mitigate the risks if possible.

If the Road Warrior did not make a food choice based on the lesser of many evils, starving was in their future, at least until they reached their final destination where other choices were available.The hamburgers may have been cold or tasted like rubber, but they served a purpose. The Road Warrior may not have even liked hamburgers! As for mitigating the risk... The Road Warrior invests in antacids.

TIPS FOR CONDUCTING A RISK/BENEFIT ANALYSIS

Don't overcomplicate the process of conducting a risk/benefit analysis. The goal is to sort out your choices and make a decision based on which one offers the most benefit and least risk.

Sometimes, the risk/benefit analysis can be done completely in your head, like the hamburger decision of the Road Warrior. When you have more time, writing down the choices and risk/benefit of each can help you do a more thorough analysis. This is particularly helpful if you are making a decision affecting your career. In this case, it may not be because both choices are bad, but you are stuck at which path you should choose.

Take out a piece of paper. Make two columns:

Risk = what's the downside of making this choice? Consider personal impact, as well as the potential impact to your family (if applicable). Consider what happens if you do not make that choice.

Benefit = what's the up side if you make this choice? Consider personal gains or family gains. Consider the long-term potential if applicable. If you make this choice, what positive thing(s) will you be able to grab that makes this decision tolerable?

That's it for a quick analysis! How many of you take the time to really think through decisions or do you whine about the lack of options?

Seek the opinions of others to better inform your risk/benefit analysis. If you only rely on your own thinking, you may be missing information that could add bullets to either column in your analysis.

Let's go back to our M-E-A-T seeking Road Warrior. Taste of the selected burger may have been revealed if the Road Warrior had asked others he saw with burger in hand. Another vendor may have offered a less rubberized product.

Here's an example:

You are a newly hired supply chain manager faced with your first decision about renewal of a vendor contract. The existing vendor used by your organization was brought into the company because of a prior relationship with one of the Vice Presidents. Based on your experience, the product offered was not in line with industry standard and seemed overpriced. Each renewal year, the Vice President would vouch for the quality of the product and the vendor and without question or external bid, the contract was renewed. This went on for the past three years prior to your hire.

The Chief Executive Officer gave you clear direction that you were to aggressively look for cost reductions and opportunities to increase the organization's competitive edge. This meant making sure everything was, at a minimum, remaining in line with industry standards. You knew of several competitive vendors offering a better product at a cheaper price. You wanted to put the renewal contract out for bid, but how do you proceed knowing the personal ties between the Vice President and the existing vendor? How do you not proceed, given the Chief Executive's mandate?

Being new, you didn't need to start your job getting on the bad side of the VP or not closing a better deal for the CEO related to quality and price. You also had not been there long enough to know the organizational culture to help inform your decision. You really felt "stuck" in which way to go.

At Risk-Getting additional renewal bids	Benefit
Alienation of VP with personal ties to existing vendor affecting future relationships	Better Quality products at a cheaper cost to the company
Disruption of services as staff work with new products	Early win with the CEO
Unknown??? Not sure of any other potential fall-out.	Proven track record of exceeding budget targets based on cost reductions, while not compromising quality, could lead to a better job in the future. Future job opportunities are what drew you to apply to this company!

DECISION! More benefits than Risks!

Mitigation Tactic (1): Meet with the VP to discuss the options and why you need to make the decision to open the process for external bids. Make sure to include the mandate from the CEO. Try to stay objective and not personalize the decision. You will gain more respect from the VP, even if they do not agree with your decision.

Mitigation Tactic (2): Include communication and education in the roll out of anything that may be a change to current practice. This should be targeted to key stakeholders- i.e., primary employees involved in using the product every day.

You may never avoid all conflict related to many decisions you may have to make throughout your career. However, thoughtful consideration of the risk and benefits of key decisions will offer you a better chance at success. This simple exercise can help in your personal life as well.

"It seems that the necessary thing to do is not to fear mistakes, to plunge in, to do the best that one can, hoping to learn enough from blunders to correct them eventually."

ABRAHAM MASLOW

"You want a valve that doesn't leak and you try everything possible to develop one. But the real world provides you with a leaky valve. You have to determine how much leakiness you can tolerate."

ARTHUR RUDOLF

6

Delays and a Time Machine

*"People say there are delays on flights. Delays, really? New York
to California in five hours, that used to take 30 years, a bunch of
people used to die on the way there, have a baby, you would end
up with a whole different group of people by the time you got there.
Now you watch a movie and [go to the toilet] and you're home."*

LOUIS C.K. (COMEDIAN)

A CLIP FROM JACKIE'S TRAVEL JOURNAL:

After a rough trip from Raleigh, N.C. into Atlanta, GA., we finally touchdown and I have exactly 20 minutes to get to my next gate. I purposefully chose a seat closer to the front of the plane so I could make the mad dash that is all too often a part of my weekly exercise routine. A quick *squat* gives me the bag under my seat. A double *overhead stretch* gives me my briefcase in the upper bin. A *head tuck* and I have avoided getting banged in the head by an anxious passenger ahead of me taking down their luggage. Multiple *twists* allow me to snake past the line of tightly packed, squirming passengers to get in a better position to make my dash to the gate. The cabin door opens, I adjust my purse and off I go, ready to *sprint* like an Olympian!

The first 5 minutes I am moving faster than sound (at least in my head). The second 5 minutes I am panting at the tram, praying it gets here soon. Once off the tram, 10 more minutes to get to the gate. I look up and of course my gate is at the extreme end of the hall. Ok, "I can do it!" I readjust everything (my bags, my mind and legs) and the sprint begins again. Five more minutes and my chest is telling me, "Slow down, fool. Who do you think you are- Jackie Joyner Kersey? A heart attack is in your future old lady. " At that moment, I think to myself, what am I doing? Listen to your chest and sit down, but I was too close to give up.

I can see the gate. I don't see a line, so I think I am too late until I actually get closer. Now all my exhaustion is replaced by sheer anger and frustration as I see "this flight has been delayed due to mechanical issues". All that running and almost dying half way down this hall and I am delayed for at least two hours! Are you serious? Other gate runners now join me with the same look of frustration on their faces. Without saying a word, we find a seat and figure out what we will do in the vacuum. It sure would be nice if a time machine could just transport us out of this craziness. No such luck, so we wait. Oh well, I wonder if Weight Watcher's on-line has the point value for the exercise routine I just completed. I needed to get something out of all of this.

CAREER LESSONS LEARNED

- Best laid plans are subject to change. In fact, all we can count on in any job is that change will be a constant. How you respond to change is within your power to control.
- Find the "pearl" in your oyster. In other words, what good can come

out of situations beyond your control? (I don't like oysters, so this analogy worked for me.) My pearl in this horrific travel experience-my mini workout.

TIPS TO MANAGING CHANGE IN THE WORKPLACE

Reconcile with yourself that you do not have the power to stop "change." You may choose to stand still; however, everything around you will continue to move forward.

Sometimes, I think we really believe if we hold our ground long enough to a belief, practice, or even, technology...our sheer will and determination will stop the change from happening. In my role as an executive consultant, I am often at the sharp end of bringing new ideas and "change" to an organization. Resistance to change is a common denominator among a portion of any staff I work with. Many try to outlast the consultant. They believe if they wait long enough, this "new" thing will pass and the organization will be on to something else or back to business as usual.

It's like those old pair of shoes we go back to because they are comfortable (already broken in) even though there is a growing hole in the sole and the style has changed dramatically since they were purchased years ago. Our mind knows we need to throw them out and get a new pair, but our heart has this connection to the past. In this instance, common sense may not be *heard* because we are operating from pure emotion. Until we are able to reconcile with that emotion so we can accept "the change," we stay stuck in the past...in our *comfort zone.* Those organizations I work with feel very comfortable with current skills even though they may be ineffective. They know things around them require a new way of working to get ahead or stay competitive, but their emotions say "stay as you are." Today's shoes don't just get holes in the soles. They get tears or cracks or holes on the shoe! Without change, there is no infrastructure left and we will soon be barefoot without investment in a new pair.

Sometimes, the reconciliation required to move forward needs to be ceremonial in order for us to say goodbye to the past.

Ceremonial ways of handling change are built into our culture, even as a child. Think of how we help children say goodbye to pets who have gone to a better place. We have mock funerals as we flush that dead goldfish to heaven. Then we buy another goldfish (something new) to allow the child to move forward. The ceremony may not completely stop the grieving process, but it does put a demonstrative end to a point in time and marks the beginning of something new. If it helps to have a ceremony over your holey shoes, go for it!

Take this same thought to the business world. Significant organizational change is often best handled with something demonstrative to mark the beginning or end of a period in time. If you are a leader in an organization, consider ceremonial change indicators. This could be as simple as pictures depicting the past, a memory wall, slogans or a kick-off celebration to announce something "new". Even if employees are still grieving the "past", the message is clear that a "new day" has arrived.

Think of all the TV ads marketing the next latest and greatest technology. They use this *ceremonial approach* to help us (the buying public) to change from our old toys to the next generation of toys. Apple does this incredibly well. Think of the rush for the next IPhone, with people spending the night in long lines to be the first to own one. This is change management at its best.

Smaller episodes of change, as shared earlier in the escapades of the Road Warrior, require a mental adjustment to get us back on track. Emotions still rule, but the reconciliation is faster because we know we have *no choice* and have a compelling reason to get it together so we can arrive at our destination safe and sound. We may whine for a bit to fellow travelers and even recall our horror story to our friends and families when we get home, but we have to get over those emotions in real time because we must get to our destination- our ultimate goal. The message is clear: we are better able to handle change when the "why" is compelling, clearly defined and we understand the ultimate goal. Ambiguity leads to more resistance and frustration.

In our everyday lives, career and personal, we are faced with changes out of our control. If we look for that compelling "why," try to understand how it could positively impact our lives and remember the ultimate goal...we may be better positioned for acceptance and moving forward.

I fully understood that I did not want to board a plane that had the slightest indication of a mechanical problem. It was an effort to keep me safe. (That's a positive!) Even though a couple hours late, I used the time to get a ton of work done, allowing me more quality time with my family when I got home. (That's another positive outcome!) I achieved the ultimate goal- getting home.

Or, we can stay emotional and fuss all night. We still may get home, but we are one miserable individual.

Change requires the will and the effort to learn new things.

Some people thrive on change and some hate change. Most don't mind change, as long as it's happening to someone else. When change gets personal, affecting our work or personal life is when that tug arrives in our gut to make a decision. *Will we engage or accept the change or will we resist?* "Will" is the operative word!

For those who love to learn and grow, change is an inevitable part of their personal and professional development. It requires a person to try new things beyond their comfort zone. The first step is always the hardest, but once you start, you discover you actually like the "new" you. You may even look back and try and remember why you had hesitation to engage in the first place. Without that will to grow, we all could still be using rotary phones, getting up to change the channels on our TV's (remote-less) and typing reports on typewriters at work.

Understand the different types of change in the workplace. Your response is directly related to the "personal impact" it may have on your career. Organizational change could be:

- **Operational**- affecting ongoing operations, like key organizational records going paperless.
- **Strategic**- reflecting a change in business direction, like a recent merger with another organization.
- **Cultural**- reflecting a change in an organization's core values, philosophies or beliefs. This could include areas like a focus on cultural diversity or including work-life blend into standards of behavior.

For example, strategic realignment with a new organizational partner may be virtually invisible, except in new name badges. However, senior leaders will need to learn how to work with a new governance model and by-laws. By comparison, implementing a paperless record requires some employees to be computer savvy and change the way they interact with organizational data. Resistance may be high in those employees who are not a part of the tech movement and embrace computer technology. They may really be quite uncomfortable with this change.

> Remember, resistance to change is very personal. Many people do not resist change; they resist change being imposed on them.

If you are the person inflicting change, **inclusion** of those it may impact prior to the change occurring is always a best practice. However, if that is not possible, clarity of the information shared- with a compelling "why" and emphasis on the ultimate goal may minimize the resistance. In addition, do not delay sharing information. Too much time between the change and the communication about the change only increases the emotion and resistance.

If you are on the receiving end of the change, take a deep breath and try to discover the "why" and the ultimate goal. Be proactive in that search if not forthcoming. Dwelling in the emotion of things you cannot change is personally destructive. Unfortunately, the ability to escape in a Time Machine is a myth.

"What does it mean to pre-board? Do you get on before you get on?"

George Carlin

7

The Undesirable Seat Buddy

"Too often travel, instead of broadening the mind,
merely lengthens the conversations."

ELIZABETH DREW

Unfortunately, on this day's travel itinerary I was stuck with the only seat left on the plane near the back. It was a small puddle jumper, with one row of seats on the left and two seats on the right. Since I am a frequent flyer, I at least got to board early and claim the luggage space above my head for my briefcase without any challenges. As I slowly found my seat, my eyes located the passenger sitting in the single seat to my left for the one hour flight (pleasant, neatly dressed and probably not the excessively talkative type that would rob me of my only nap before a long day at work)- one traveler down and one more to go. We exchanged smiles and settled in for the ride.

Then we both looked up at the same time, prompted by the strong smell of body odor coming from the front of the plane. We saw a heavily garbed woman working her way to the back. Without saying a word, our eyes locked again as we said the traveler's prayer- "please don't let her sit next to me." Today, I drew the unlucky straw. That empty seat next to mine belonged to her. This was going to be a long, miserable 1 hour flight. There was nowhere to go, no empty seat and I was stuck with the *undesirable seat buddy.*

The adjustments throughout this trip were numerous. I tried turning my body into the aisle, placing a napkin over my nose, repeated trips to the restroom for air and pretending to stretch my legs until I had to buckle up for landing. My buddy to the left, in the single seat, even joined me for relief- the smells crossing the aisle. My undesirable seat buddy seemed totally unaware of the impact she was having on us and fell asleep shortly after take-off. The flight attendant told us, "Hold on, the flight will be over soon". The funny thing about that was we never said a word to her either about our dilemma. She knew.

When I finally got to my hotel, I changed clothes and took a shower to relieve myself of the odors I was sure had permeated my very being. I bagged and tightly sealed my clothes for my return trip and prayed to never have that happen to me again. In this circumstance, I could escape- never to see my undesirable seat buddy again (I hope). But it did make me think about all those we may encounter that there is really no escape pod. I am sure you have all experienced people you work with that you have no choice but to interact with on a daily basis. They may even be seated right next to you. Short term adjustments are not an option. What do you do now? We can't change jobs every time we must work with people we don't care for.

Career Lessons Learned

- We cannot choose our coworkers, but we can choose how we interact with them.

- Elevate commonalities
- Explore differences
- Respectfully confront tensions to enhance workplace relationships
- Leadership has the opportunity to take multiple variables into consideration to align employees with corporate culture upon hire.

TIPS TO MOVING COWORKERS FROM UNDESIRABLE TO DESIRABLE (OR AT LEAST TOLERABLE)

Say to yourself, "Work is work and home is home. Friendships are a bonus at work and sought at home. I do not have to love my co-workers, but I do need to respect them and learn how to co-exist with them in the workplace."

How many of us actually choose our place of employment for the social networking aspect of the job? Not many. Most of us seek employment to fulfill our career aspirations or to earn a living wage. We are delighted when friendships transcend the day to day workplace into our personal lives. But, it is not our ultimate goal of work. So, why are we surprised when we encounter an *undesirable seat buddy*? We did not choose them and both of us may have approached work with different core values and work ethic. Survival and hopefully finding joy at work will depend on the ability and desire to dwell more on shared values than differences with our coworkers.

Beware of assumptions about your "seat buddies" –listen and seek to understand

If a coworker has achieved the label of "undesirable", then we have already arrived at a set of assumptions about them in our heads. We may have even shared those assumptions with others, spreading the "undesirable" perception to others in the workplace. Some of us may have been the victim to that title during some part of our career. Usually, there is some grain of fact threaded through assumptions. Unfortunately, the context of those facts may be lost without dialogue with the one labeled undesirable.

For instance, if we are offended by an obese coworker because of their weight, we may harbor assumptions about their work ethic. They may also receive the label as lazy and slow. Without getting to know that person, we would never know their weight is the result of an endocrine issue and that they actually have above average technical skills to do the job. That coworker is not obligated to share the information above. However, if we listen first and ground our assumptions in facts acquired during relationship building, we may reach a different conclusion. They may not be so undesirable after all.

What assumptions have been made about you in the workplace that you wished someone had just asked you about? Remember, we bring our whole selves to work...including our emotions. Protracted periods of anger, depression or withdrawal could push a person into that undesirable category. They also could be driven by a pending divorce, economic challenges or a significant loss. These are all other parts of our lives we may choose not to share. However, if a caring person just asked if I was okay, I may have shared that I had things going on at home and previous assumptions may have changed. I may have at least moved into the tolerable category.

> If the undesirable turns into the unbearable, seek help if a one to one conversation with that individual is not possible in order to resolve what challenges you. Approach BEFORE the situation turns unbearable if possible. Both confrontations will take courage and respectful truth-telling.

Conflict is a normal part of any healthy relationship. After all, two people can't be expected to agree on everything, all the time. Learning how to deal with conflict – rather than avoiding it – is crucial. When conflict is mismanaged, it can cause great harm to a relationship, but when handled in a respectful, positive way, conflict provides an opportunity to strengthen the bond between two people.

Conflict arises from differences, both large and small. It occurs whenever people disagree over their values, motivations, perceptions, ideas, or desires. Sometimes these differences appear trivial, but when a conflict triggers strong feelings, a deep personal need is often at the core of the problem. These needs can be a need to feel safe and secure or a need to feel respected and valued. Our perceptions are influenced by our life experiences, culture, values, and beliefs.

The needs of both parties play important roles in the long-term success of most relationships, and each deserves respect and consideration. In personal relationships, a lack of understanding about differing needs can result in distance, arguments, and break-ups. In workplace conflicts, differing needs are often at the heart of bitter disputes, sometimes resulting in broken deals, fewer profits and lost jobs. When you can recognize the legitimacy of conflicting needs and become willing to examine them in an environment of compassionate understanding, it opens pathways to creative problem solving, team building, and improved relationships.

Here are some things to remember about conflicts as you take your next step toward resolution with your undesirable seat buddy.

1. **Conflicts continue to fester when ignored.** Because conflicts involve perceived threats to our well-being and survival, they stay with us until we face and resolve them.

2. **Conflicts are an opportunity for growth.** When you're able to resolve conflict in a relationship, it builds trust. You can feel secure knowing your relationship can survive challenges and disagreements.

3. **Successful conflict resolution depends on your ability to regulate stress and your emotions.**

If you can reframe your thinking to approach your undesirable seat buddy for a **private** talk to improve your working relationship:

- **Remain calm, non-defensive and respectful (as you would likely want someone to approach you).** By staying calm, you can accurately read and interpret verbal and nonverbal communication. When you're in control of your emotions, you can communicate your needs without threatening, frightening, or punishing others. By avoiding disrespectful words and actions, you can almost always resolve a problem faster.

- **Find a private location for the meeting and don't broadcast it to other coworkers.**
- **Be ready to listen, forgive (if appropriate) and be ready to move past any bad feelings without holding resentments or anger.**
- **Be willing to compromise.**
- **If you have no "will" to listen or accept a change in your perceptions, don't go into this discussion alone. Ask for a facilitator.** This is usually your supervisor, especially if it impacts your work. Someone from Human Resources can also serve in this role.
- **Seek to really understand the source of the conflict from both sides.**
- **Communicate clearly.**
- **Be aware of non-verbal communication, often the most important ingredient in conflict resolution.** That includes: facial expressions, posture, gesture, pace, tone and intensity of voice.
- **Make conflict resolution the priority rather than winning or "being right."** Maintaining and strengthening the relationship, rather than "winning" the argument, should always be your first priority.

If in a leadership role- consider peer interviewing of new hires using behavioral-based questions to select the "right" match for the organizational culture. Peer inclusion in the process helps to minimize the undesirable seat buddy syndrome. The benefits of peer interviewing include:

- Applicants are more likely to let their guard down with peers, so the organization will get a better sense of who their candidates are and how they'll fit.
- Employees help to select their future coworkers. Being involved in the selection process is good for morale and productivity; employees now have more of a stake in the organization. All this strengthens workers' commitment to the organization and

builds on a community atmosphere, in which peoples' opinions do matter.

- As employees are invested in the new hires' success (they've already met them and have a sense of who they are), they are more likely to help new employees. Similarly, new employees start work knowing that their peers support them.

"I can't promise you a perfect relationship, but what I can promise you is that as long as we are trying- I am staying".

ANONYMOUS AUTHOR

"Putting your love, trust, and understanding to each other little by little, day by day is the perfect recipe for a stronger relationship".

JAY GUILLERMO

8

Head in the Clouds

"Like all great travelers, I have seen more than I remember, and remember more than I have seen."

BENJAMIN DISRAELI

"Travel can be one of the most rewarding forms of introspection."

LAWRENCE DURRELL

About 20 minutes after take-off, I slowly open the window shade to see the most beautiful clouds surrounding the airplane like giant pillows made of marshmallow filling. When I am not absorbed in work or so tired I can't see straight (often the plight of a Road Warrior), I let my mind drift among those clouds to distant places forgotten during a busy day. Sometimes, I see shapes and faces that remind me of people important in my life. Some days I can even see myself stretched out on a cloud taking in the vast beauty around me. No, I am not crazy, nor have I gone over the edge. I just allowed myself to let go of all the stress of the day and relax into the moment. I put "Work Jackie" to bed, and allowed "Creative Jackie" to engage.

In our work or personal life, how often do we actually allow ourselves a pause to **think or dream?** Most of us are in constant "doing mode." In other words, we are always in motion to do something or go somewhere ...sometimes without knowing if we really are achieving an outcome or benefit for our actions. Many proceed through the day on automatic pilot. We are tethered to our electronic devices and our brains are exposed to constant data input. TV, cell phones, IPADS, and laptops help us to stay in that "doing mode." We TWEET or text, some even taking those devices to bed with them. Where is the off button? When do we allow ourselves to just "be" and turn on our creative minds to plan, think, dream or here's a novel thought...do nothing but float on the clouds appreciating the beauty around us and those sharing it with us. We complain about not having enough time, when the real issue is: "How do we spend the time we have?"

CAREER LESSONS LEARNED

- Everyone needs time throughout the work week to pause, think and breathe.
- Constant "doing" may only yield exhaustion and not results. Quality work is not found when one is in constant motion.
- The investment in a "time to plan" or "re-evaluate actions to date" may actually yield better results and time left over to exhale.

TIPS TO ADDING CLOUD FLOATING TO YOUR PORTFOLIO

Proactively hit the pause button to add clarity and focus to your work.

I am certain many of you reading this are thinking, "Is she nuts? I can't just pause during my workday without my boss hitting the pause button on my employment!" That's because you are thinking in large amounts of time and you may not be including the time you have to pause during lunch or breaks.

If you find yourself mentally blocked or not as productive, take five or an early break to clear your head. Take a walk (without your electronic toys) or just close your door (if you have one) and go to a place that makes you happy- in your head. Do some cloud floating. You will be surprised that a short mental escape will help to get you back on track and you actually may have more energy and focus to complete the work in front of you.

But, that's not our reality is it? It is not unusual to see everyone with their heads bent forward reading email messages or texting with fury on breaks and over lunch. We can't even walk down the street without talking on our phones. There are recent news stories about people falling into fountains, walking into walls and off curbs because they were distracted by texting or talking on the phone. We can't even disconnect when we are driving. Our doing button stuck in the "on" position. What on earth did we do before we had this technology? I think we actually took a break, enjoyed our meals and had conversations (including eye contact) with those around us. I think we actually had time to dream and breathe.

Do a gut check- are most of your waking hours "on" or in "doing mode"? What impact has it had on your work life and personal life? What are you willing to change or give up in order to add more cloud floating into your portfolio?

Once a quarter, check your "doing" list. Do your actions on a daily basis help you achieve your goals or are they just taking your energy and time away from just "being"? Being= time for self- reflection, time for creative thinking, time for family and friends, time to float among the clouds. Readjust your "doing" list as appropriate.

Does quiet time make you uncomfortable? The answer for many may be "YES"! That's probably because we don't do it enough for it to be comfortable in the "off" mode. For example, how many days does it take when you finally are on vacation to get work and deadlines out of your mind? I know for me, it's about 3-4 straight days and then it's almost time to return to work. I love the escape of a cruise because I have no choice but to unplug from technology. However you get there, you need to gain comfort in the "off" mode. Here are some ways to consider increasing your skill in this area:

- Meditation/Yoga
- Exercise- especially those that are aerobic in nature
- Outdoor activity- try and really see the beauty in the world around you
- Meaningful dialogue with friends and family- look into their eyes
- Escape in the pages of a great book
- Listen to the music- really listen and float on a cloud

Add planning time into your work life schedule. This is an essential ingredient for successful leaders.

Planning (also called **forethought**) is the process of thinking about and organizing the activities required to achieve a desired goal. There are personal plans and organizational plans. One is more about how you prioritize your "doing" list every day and the other is about how leaders stay focused on the important things. Planning always has a purpose. The purpose may be achievement of certain goals or targets.

Here's a recipe for prioritizing your work daily:

- At the start of your day, hit the pause button to organize how you will approach the day. This can be a mental or quick written check list. Start with those things out of your control (times, deliverables, meetings). They go to the top of your list.
- Prioritize the rest of your tasks. Figure out what needs to be done now, what needs to be done before the end of the day and what can be completed another day.
- Schedule your day according to your priorities. If you need to finish a task/project as soon as possible, set aside enough time at the beginning of your day to complete this task.

- Take your work habits into account. Prioritizing and scheduling is one thing, but making that work within your own schedule is an entirely different matter. If you tend to focus better on tasks before lunch, make sure that all of your complicated tasks are completed before this time. If you are more productive an hour before the close of your business day, use this time to get your important tasks done. Understanding how you work can help you be more efficient and increase your productivity.

- Write down anything that did not get accomplished during your day, and make it a priority for your next day's list of tasks. While we would all love to finish our to-do lists at the day's end, it is not always possible. Prioritizing the previous day's unfinished tasks will prevent them from getting forgotten as the new day brings new challenges.

- Don't forget your cloud floating time! Take a break and your lunch. Breathe, daydream and allow your creative self to surface.

For those in leadership roles, think about your primary goals and objectives needed to drive organizational results. Have you set aside enough time in your daily activities to assure your plans and actions are appropriate and on target? Are new plans needed to course correct based on current results? Certain plans may even need your creative side to engage. Here are some additional considerations:

- Hit the pause button at least every ninety days to assess organizational goals within your span of control against results to date. Do your current actions align or are you just "doing."

- At least weekly, schedule sixty- ninety minutes with yourself to "think." Leaders must have a designated time to think and plan in order to effectively do their jobs. Sixty- ninety minutes once a week is barely enough, but more than most leaders give themselves.

- Are you assuming actions that are really the job of a direct report? What actions do you need to take in order to let go and have them be more accountable for successful execution?

Encourage cloud floating to others around you. Role model this healthy attribute to a well-balanced workforce. The results will amaze for the organization and you!

Nonstop work—without sufficient downtime for family, friends, and solitude—violates the natural rhythms of life and nature. I remember a former supervisor, who was a perfectionist: obsessive, competitive, extremely mission-driven, and excessively failure-aversive. These traits made it difficult for her to set healthy boundaries between work and the rest of her life. And those traits affected not just her life but also the lives of all the members of the team.

Technology and non-stop internet connections have compounded these tendencies in driven people, enabling them to work nonstop and to drive their subordinates to do the same. The depressed economy has made things worse still, leading many workers feeling vulnerable to job loss and pressured to work harder (sometimes at home).

A lot of people assume that the key to productivity is hard work, and of course hard work is essential. But there are limits to how much work is useful. Working harder and longer doesn't necessarily mean getting more done or that the results achieved will be better.

You may have heard of several studies that show the power of mid-day brief catnaps in improving learning, memory, and creative thinking. It was shown that napping makes people more effective problem-solvers. Some companies, such as Google, have even created nap rooms where their employees can catch some restorative shuteye during the workday.

Probably the most feasible and easily implemented approach to reaping the benefits of cloud floating is to seize time off regularly, whenever you can. Modest changes in the routine of work would allow a busy multi-tasker to slow down, recharge, and return to work with more focus, energy, and creativity. There are numerous ways to add more cloud floating time into a busy life, including work-free weekends, post-lunch catnaps, days off, vacations from technology, no-work evenings, and regular 10-minute work breaks.

And, those in leadership roles should role model these healthy work-life behaviors to their staff. Most workaholics focus so much on finishing the projects in front of them that they do not strategize, prioritize, or seek more creative solutions. It is the later that will drive sustainable organizational results for the future. Cloud floating should be added to performance expectations...imagine that!

"Clouds come floating into my life, no longer to carry rain or usher storm, but to add color to my sunset sky."

Rabindranath Tagore

"It is a very beautiful day. The woman looks around and thinks: there cannot ever have been a spring more beautiful than this. I did not know until now that clouds could be like this. I did not know that the sky is the sea and that clouds are the souls of happy ships, sunk long ago. I did not know that the wind could be tender, like hands as they caress–what did I know–until now?"

Unica Zürn

9

Touchdown

"You define a good flight by negatives: you didn't get hijacked,
you didn't crash, you didn't throw up, you weren't late, and
you weren't nauseated by the food. So you are grateful."

PAUL THEROUX

The pilot's voice comes over the loud speaker, "We are 100 miles from the Miami International Airport. Please make sure your seat belt is securely fastened, tray tables are in their up and locked position and begin to shut off all electronic devices. We are anticipating some turbulence upon approach to the Miami Airport. Flight attendants, please prepare the cabin for landing." You take a deep breath and begin to get mentally prepared to have your stomach do flip flops through the bumpy touchdown.

No matter how many flight miles you have racked up, touchdown still has this effect on you. I am not sure if it is the actual turbulence that makes you sick or the unknown of how bad it could be. It also could dredge up memories from the back of your mind about that really bad flight you were on 5 years ago. No matter the source, we join all the other passengers anxiously anticipating touchdown. And, by no means is this just an issue for women. I have witnessed the manliest of men gripping their seats or closing their eyes.

Once the plane finally hits, you can hear cheers from some (thankful for surviving), others may groan at the skill of the pilot and others move on-quickly gathering their belongings ready for the next adventure. Do any of these reactions sound vaguely familiar as it relates to how we deal with the unknown in the workplace? When we don't know what's exactly coming around the corner- a new leader, new processes or new performance expectations- our guts churn, we whine about the wisdom of leadership and some embrace the unknown.

So many variables can be the source of our fear- with change hitting the top of the list. However, what takes our fear to another level is when we are void of information or details of the change, allowing our emotions to paint the picture in our minds. Emotional paint brushes are always flawed. If our emotional perspectives are shared with others on staff, we could cause fear to spread rapidly throughout the organization with very little facts to substantiate the escalation. The original turbulence has now been converted to **organizational gossip**.

During my 30 plus year career, I think I have experienced all kinds of organizational turbulence. As a leader, I may have even been the perceived source of the turbulence. Here's an example of turbulence gone wild!

A major health system was undergoing significant challenges as it went from a single 600 bed medical facility to merging with three other area hospitals. The merger took almost a year to be finalized after the initial contracts were signed. Today, mergers and acquisitions are quite common throughout the country. However, the cultural change required of all involved are always difficult and communication internally and externally is never enough. This was definitely the case with this newly formed health system.

Executive Leadership carefully worded sporadic communication to staff and the general public about the merger and changes to come. Questions and stories began to fly. The range of organizational gossip went from CEO impropriety, financial ruin, physician uprising, and anything else your mind can think of (none of which were true). The real facts were more about growth and future viability of all the organizations involved...a good and not a bad thing. However, the length of time it took for the merger to reach a successful settlement, void of adequate communication, left a huge amount of time for the organizational gossip to get out of control. This organization spent a year following the merger rebuilding a tarnished reputation and gaining internal trust. Again stories were not based on facts, but fear of the unknown.

CAREER LESSONS LEARNED

- **Change or fear of the unknown can cause people to feel insecure about their jobs.** They aren't quite sure what's going to happen with the organization. As a result they might gossip, speculate, or spread false rumors. This is human nature's way of coping; people are trying to understand and gather information so they feel safe.
- **Not all employees will respond to the unknown in the same way.** They may share the initial shock of something new (anticipated turbulence); however, some may embrace changes to come.
- **Leaders should always err on the side of over-communication, especially as it relates to any organizational turbulence.**

TIPS TO SURVIVING ORGANIZATIONAL TURBULENCE

Leaders have primary responsibility to manage organizational turbulence. Here are some tips for leaders:

- **Set the record straight.** A lot of gossip happens during the "unknown." As a leader, be as transparent and authentic as possible with information.

- **Don't believe the gossip you hear.** Sometimes when people start telling stories, it's easy to believe they are real. This can damage trust and relationships. Remember you are only hearing part of the story.
- **Open your door.** Have an open door policy where people can ask you questions. If people aren't asking questions, they aren't feeling safe — something you might want to examine as a leader.
- **Say "I don't know."** When you don't know the answer to something, say so. And recognize that if you say "*I don't know*," people will be scared because we don't feel safe with not knowing.

When going through organizational change, be just as vigilant on communication strategies as operational strategies. Appoint a Communication's Officer for significant change (i.e., leadership, mergers...). Think internal and external communication strategies. Nothing will stay inside the walls of the organization, even if confidentiality clauses are in effect. Count on leaks to the general public.

Here are some tips for the employee:

- **Accept turbulence as a way of life.** Like the Road Warrior who has thousands of flight miles, turbulence is a part of the expected flight plan.
- **Be aware of your surroundings.** Recognizing that change happens is desirable. It's even better, though, to recognize when change might be occurring in your own specific situation. Keep alert to subtle clues. For example, are you being excluded from important meetings? Does your boss seem more distant? Is the rumor mill engaged?
- **Recognize you may go through stages once turbulence takes hold.** Reactions to organizational change can resemble those to the death of a loved one. The early stages include shock and denial (refusing to believe what has happened and instead believing everything will be all right), guilt (at not having done or said more), and anger (usually at leadership). Later, one passes through the stages

of acceptance (acknowledging what has happened) and moving on. With respect to organizational change, an additional "negotiations" stage can occur, in which the affected person offers to work harder as a way of preventing or forestalling the change.

- All the stages don't necessarily occur. The progression might not be a smooth linear one, and different amounts of time may be involved with the different stages. Regardless, the quicker you get to the acceptance and moving on stages, the better it will be for you.

- **Keep talking! Trust but verify incoming information.** Communication is always important, but especially so when you face organizational turbulence. A lack of communications from others can have a negative impact, while effective communications can have a positive one. Don't just sit back and wait for things to happen. Talk to your boss, your boss's boss, and your co-workers to get their understanding. When dealing with co-workers, however, be aware that news can be distorted and can be mixed with rumor. Talk to others who have undergone such a change. What difficulties did they experience and how did they deal with them? How can you adapt their experiences to your own situation?

- **Stay open to a positive outcome. Do a self-check on what you bring to a new situation.** Sometimes, even though we may have anticipated a negative outcome, we actually may be surprised. Our plane landed without incident, no turbulence at all. For example, if there are changes in organizational structure affecting your current job, take a look at the requirements of the new situation. Maybe your current job doesn't fit exactly into it. However, what skills, from your old role, *can* you apply to the new situation? In other words, instead of focusing on differences, focus on similarities. How can you adapt your skills to the new situation in front of you to create a softer landing?

- **Check your attitude when you deplane.** In other words, once the turbulence passes, are you in a positive or negative space? Look for opportunities and become involved, if applicable. It will hasten your adjustment to organizational turbulence.

"When you come out of the storm, you won't be the same person who walked in. That's what this storm's all about."

HARUKI MURAKAMI

""There is bound to be turbulence in the clouds of confusion before one can view the friendly skies, and an illuminated landing strip."

T.F. HODGE

10

Cultural Reset

"Certainly, travel is more than the seeing of sights; it is a change that goes on, deep and permanent, in the ideas of living."

MIRIAM BEARD

"Traveling, you realize that differences are lost: each city takes to resembling all cities, places exchange their form, order, distances, a shapeless dust cloud invades the continents."

ITALO CALVINO

As the plane door opens to allow exit from its tubular chamber, I already know this is not home. The humidity hit me as soon as one foot touches the jetway. I can already feel my hair beginning to swell as this new environment lets me know this will not be a good hair week. Even though I dressed in light garb, perspiration begins to gather on my forehead, hands and down my back. You hear the flight attendant say, "Welcome to sunny Florida."

Leaving the jet way, you hear the bustle of people trying to get to their connecting flights or just out of the airport. You hear the Latin dialect, now a norm to this part of the lower southeast. You see signs with Spanish as the dominant language and food vendors offering a variety of culinary specialties not common in other parts of the country and certainly not the southern cuisine of North Carolina!

As I make my way to baggage claim, I am stopped twice by other travelers speaking Spanish to me, I think asking for directions or help. (They believe I am of Latin descent because of my exterior presentation.) I do not speak Spanish; however, can usually understand what people are saying. With the multi-cultural changes happening all over the country, I have often wondered if learning Spanish would be something I should pursue. At my age, I am not sure I am up for that growth experience. I have gotten by all these years with my native language, why should I change now? My grandchildren will probably have to learn other languages just to survive in the rapidly changing culture in the Unites States. We already see job posting, where being multi-lingual is either required or preferred.

My **cultural reset** continues as I leave the airport and arrive at my hotel- home for the next few days... this time my adjustments are not about language or the weather, just about how things are done. I quickly have to figure out where I will eat, transportation and do I have enough shampoo, conditioner and toothpaste. For a Road Warrior, these types of cultural resets can be experienced weekly. They need to quickly acclimate to their new environment in order to be effective in the job they have been sent to do.

We all experience cultural resets in our work lives. From the moment we are hired, our cultural reset begins. New organizational culture, leaders, co-workers and even our new workspace require a personal readjustment. For those who had to relocate for employment, the reset may resemble that of the aforementioned Road Warrior. Our ability and willingness to acclimate to our new work place reality or do a cultural reset directly correlates with our success in the workplace. (Of course, job selection based on cultural fit makes this transition much easier to achieve.)

Cultural resets are also required following the numerous organizational changes that occur throughout your employment. Race or ethnicity is often what comes to mind when one thinks of "culture." However culture is so much more.

Career Lessons Learned

- Cultural resets are reoccurring requirements in the workplace.
- Choose cultural fit wisely before accepting a new job. Prevention is better than a forced acceptance once hired.
- Think broader than race or ethnicity when thinking of culture. Cultural resets will include acclimating to a variety of people different than ourselves, organizational dynamics and new environments.
- Cultural resets do not require you to lose your own identity, just to be open to something new with respectful engagement.

Tips for a Successful Cultural Reset

Do your homework before accepting a job. In this high-tech age, there is so much available on the internet to give you a sense of organizational culture. During an interview ask questions about:

- Corporate culture/Strategic priorities
- Healthcare and other benefits
- Financial planning and retirement
- Ob-Boarding/Expectations for the first 90 days of employment
- Continuing your education
- Ongoing career path

Understand the different types of cultural reset that may be required of you. Be prepared to take a good hard look in the mirror to do a self –check on how you may be affected. Remember, our response to culture is very personal and varies according to past experiences, preconceived notions about the unknown and even how we were raised. Your success in cultural reset will depend on how honest you are with your own starting point and how open you are to differences that may take you out of your comfort zone.

Variables That May Trigger A Cultural Reset

Cultural variables:
- Gender
- Age
- Ethnicity
- Race
- Sexual Orientation
- Educational Background
- Religion
- Physical/mental ability
- Military/veteran status
- Lifestyle
- Immigrant status
- Language facility
- Communication styles

Functional variables, the way we:
- Think
- Learn
- Process information
- Respond to authority
- Show respect
- Reach Agreements
- Communicate with each other (Myers Briggs)

Historical variables
- Family make-up
- Perspective
- Political outlook
- Intergroup relationships

> **Organizational variables**
> - Leadership changes
> - Mergers and acquisitions
> - Financial challenges
> - New programs or work processes
> - New technology/tools

Assimilation is not required. The excerpt below from my book, "The Yellow Suit-A Guide for Women in Leadership" offers great insight into this tip.

One month on the job and my first Leadership meeting, as I entered the Board room I saw one of the largest board tables I have ever seen, enough to seat more than 25 leaders. Each leader moved to a seat and as I moved to one nearest the door, the Regional President asked for me to sit next to him, dead center. My immediate boss sat directly across from me. No one had told me the rules for this meeting, especially the unspoken rule that you never question anything the Regional President said. I was definitely in for a surprise when I crossed over into forbidden territory respectfully challenging some information presented by our Regional President.

For a major portion of my career, I had taught fundraising in the non-profit arena- a skill not often shared by other Health System CEO's. As our Regional President presented the action plan and challenges, I felt compelled to offer some differing insight that may be a more effective approach. The more I talked, the more the room got silent, with even some team members gasping as if I had committed a crime. I felt my boss kick me under the table to save me from myself and the anticipated wrath of the Regional President. It was too late. The words had left my lips. I had presented an alternative approach, offered factually for his consideration.

When I was done, no one except the Regional President would give me eye contact. It was as if they all knew I was going to be handed my job of one month in my hand and sent packing out the door. Even my boss had slouched down in his chair, head in hand. After a brief pause, the Regional President smiled and said, "I like your spunk and your recommendations are on target with where we want to go. Let's amend this plan to incorporate Jackie's action steps."

The next thing I heard was a collective sigh and one by one, eye contact resumed accompanied by nods of approval. My boss even sat straight up in his chair with the biggest grin, as if to say, "she works for me!" After the meeting I was surprised to get several thank-you notes from leaders in the group. They all had the same theme about being a courageous professional who had changed the cultural norm of the leadership team. Wow! Assimilation was not required...professionalism was the key.

In the face of "group think" we might be tempted to go with the flow and not make waves. The path of least resistance is saying "yes" when you want to say "no" and that road is always paved with regrets and mistakes. While compromise is good and a necessary part of healthy relationships in the workplace, no one should have to fully deny their feelings or thoughts and remain voiceless. You can stay true to your principles, responding factually and respectfully.

When faced with a cultural reset with coworkers ask yourself the following questions:

- **Do you have humility with regard to someone who is different than yourself, or do you maintain a sense of arrogance?** In other words...because you have certain characteristics...do those characteristics make you better than another person or just different? And, shouldn't you respect those differences?
- **Are you willing to listen verses pushing your way?** Oftentimes when we think we are better...we try to influence others that our way is the right way? Does that block how you view another's belief or practice?
- **Are you open to changing based on new experiences verses standing on old beliefs that may not be grounded in today's reality.** How many people today hold onto the past...past impressions...what our parents taught us to believe about others that may be misperceptions about an entire culture or people? How would that influence how you interact with your co-workers?

- There's an old saying..."you don't know...what you don't know." We may not know all the cultural nuances for people we work with ... but we need to have the wisdom to ask appropriate questions and the openness to change or revise our traditional views in order to be effective.

Three small pebbles to keep in your pocket with regard to cultural reset:
- Relax and leave yourself open to change
- Listen with your ears and heart
- Seek to understand

Cultural reset will be uncomfortable at first. Think of it as a growth spurt!

"Most people do not listen with the intent to understand; they listen with the intent to reply."

STEPHEN R. COVEY

"I'm bilingual, speaking English and body language. I prefer the latter, because I can speak it silently and without listening and while my back is turned. "

JAROD KINTZ

11

GPS- My Mandatory Accessory

*"The best way to follow your dreams, is to put
GPS on the back of your eye lids."*
MICHAEL PHELPS

*"Lifewithout purpose is like driving without GPS making all the wrong
turns, in the wrong lane taking double the time to get on the right track."*
AUTHOR UNKNOWN

Thank God for this little box that knows I am terrible with directions and yells them out to me in short bursts as I make my way to my next destination. (My husband tells me that when I have the inclination to go right- go left and I will probably be headed in the right direction.) Every city seems to look the same these days. Even street names seem to recycle. The voice coming from the box is irritating and sometimes makes me feel like a complete idiot, "*Recalculating*" as I fail to adhere to the specific instructions outlined on the screen. I am not exactly sure when this little gizmo was invented, but it had to be either someone's Mom or an autocratic business man with an edge doing the voice overs. Like a little sheep, I follow. Why? Because I need to get where I am expected to be, by a certain time and I trust the technology knows better than I.

GPS stands for "Global Positioning System." It is a space-based satellite navigation system that provides location and time information in all weather conditions, anywhere on or near the Earth where there is an unobstructed line of sight to GPS satellites. Our small boxes receive up to date information from these satellites which gives us turn by turn instructions to get us from one location to another. If land maps change, the satellite is adjusted and new information is sent to us to make sure we don't turn down a street that is blocked by construction or is no longer accessible. Periodic adjustments/updates are made by smart people in an office somewhere (not aliens in the sky).

Believe it or not, all organizations have some form of a GPS. Some are more formal than others, but there is a road map. And, like the GPS, there are business men and women sitting in an office somewhere readjusting the signals to their workforce to drive results. They look retrospectively at organizational performance to determine which way to go and prospectively at things to come that may impede progress. Then they set the turn by turn instructions. And, for the most part, we trust their expertise in making the best decisions for the viability of the place we rely on for a living wage.

If we make a wrong turn on the organizational road, our leaders yell, "Recalculating." Sometimes, we are allowed to just course correct (with some help). New turn by turn directions may be created and shared for us to execute. If we refuse to execute, we may find ourselves in a ditch-unemployed.

CAREER LESSONS LEARNED

- All organizations need a GPS to reach their strategic goals and sustain viability for the future.

- An organizational GPS offers employees turn by turn instructions on how to execute on specific goals. They must be thoughtful, communicated with clarity and flexible enough to allow for course corrections throughout the organization's journey. Leadership must periodically pause to check for accuracy of data loaded into the GPS and update as needed.

- Once employees understand the organization's road map, compliance with the turn by turn instructions become a matter of skill or will. Do you have the skill to complete the task? Do you want to complete the task (will)? There may be training, like driver's education, if skill is the issue. And, there will be price to pay for noncompliance. Think of it as your "toll."

TIPS FOR STAYING ON THE ROAD TO SUCCESS

Know your organization's road map!

The organizational road map is often found in their strategic plan. After working with the Board of Directors, Executive leadership is charged to develop more specific plans that help to achieve the targeted goals. That's where you come in! Most strategic plans are shared with employees, even if at a high-level. You will be responsible to execute on what has been decided.

Unfortunately, this is usually the part during a CEO presentation, when we allow our thoughts to drift to other places, thinking *"this level of information is not necessary for me to know."* Some of us may even take this as an opportunity to "cloud float." Get off the cloud, for now, and get your head back into the overview. Try to understand the strategic priorities of the organization. Take notes and ask questions of your supervisor to clarify anything you do not understand, especially those strategic goals that directly will impact your work.

Assess your current skill set against the organizational strategic priorities. Proactively seek training for gaps in skills.

Proactive is the operative word in the above statement. Don't wait to be found obsolete. That means staying aware of what's happening around you. Like the road warrior trying to navigate in a new city, employees must be alert to what is current organizational reality, challenges for the future and potential response. You may not be able to get inside the heads of leadership for the answers, but you do have access to television, newspapers and possibly a pulse on the community buzz. For instance, how long have we known about the planned changes related to health care reform? For those working in the health care field, did you look carefully with a discerning eye at the impact those changes will have on your work and place of employment or did you just think about health care reform from a "personal impact" perspective? Employees must pay attention to the road signs and stay professionally current to make sure you remain valued going forward.

Know the organizational "rules" of the road.

Most organizations have a Code of Conduct or Standards of Behavior. We usually sign them upon hire and put them in a file or drawer never to be thought of again. They usually include things like the dress code or absentee policies. Like the stop signs on the roads traveled by a Road Warrior, they are the organizational stop signs. Employees who choose to run a stop sign or violate the standards face consequences through a standard policy, such as a progressive discipline system, which has grave consequences for the most serious violations. Also, employees may get a warning for the first occurrence of a less-serious violation, but they would get a more severe consequence for another occurrence of the same behavior. Progressive discipline gives employees a chance to change their behavior and continue employment. These standards are the mandatory conditions of employment. Do you know your organization's standards of behavior?

Here's a list of what could be included in an organization's standards of behavior:

- Safety
- Fitness for Duty
- Use of Alcohol
- Attendance Reporting
- Harassment and Discrimination
- Workplace Violence
- Weapons in the Workplace
- Gambling in the Workplace
- Company Assets
- Computer and System Security
- Social Media
- Company Records
- Records Retention
- Confidential and Customer-Specific Information
- Supplier Code of Conduct
- Employee Privacy
- Business Expenses
- Corporate Name, Logo, and Colors
- Publishing Articles
- Endorsements
- Community Activities
- News Media Inquiries
- Employment Inquiries

It is leadership's responsibility to ensure that employees are aware of the organization's values, ethics, expectations and what the organizational "rules of the road" are throughout their employment. Leaders must also role model this behavior. When leader's role model expected behavior, they create an environment of high morale, good principles and respect for the organization among employees.

Seek new employment if your values do not align with the new organizational direction. Don't wait to pay a "toll" for non-compliance. Termination does not look good on anyone's resume.

There are some people who live in a dream world, and there are some who face reality; and then there are those who turn one into the other."

DOUGLAS H. EVERETT

"Plans are only good intentions unless they immediately degenerate into hard work."

PETER DRUCKER

STRATEGIC PLANS 101

Strategic plans usually address one or more of the following questions:

1. What do we do?
2. For whom do we do it?
3. How do we excel?

The key components of a strategic plan include a description of an organization's vision, mission, values and strategies.

Vision: outlines what the organization wants to be, or how it wants the world in which it operates to be.

Mission: Defines the fundamental purpose of an organization or an enterprise, succinctly describing why it exists and what it does to achieve its vision.

Values: Beliefs that are shared among the stakeholders of an organization.

Strategy: Goals for which the organization is striving and the policies by which it requires to get there. A strategy is sometimes called a roadmap–which is the path chosen to get to the end vision.

"By failing to prepare, you are preparing to fail."

BENJAMIN FRANKLIN

Strategy is followed by specific actions needed to achieve the desired results.

12

Shampoo, Conditioner and Soap

"You never know when some small thing will lead to a big idea. Travel is very inspirational–but it's in the ordinary that I find my themes of love and work and family."

ADRIANA TRIGIANI

"Travel works best when you're forced to come to terms with the place you're in."

PAUL THEROUX

I am barely off the elevator and that familiar smell hits my nose as I make my way to my room- whatever they use to clean hotel rooms, the chlorine from the indoor pool and people smells. The older the hotel, the stronger this smell seems to ascend from the walls and carpet. Even if not visibly unclean, the smells hang on like little footprints from all the hotel visitors that have come before me. I must admit, my sensitivity may be heightened sense I am on the road so much. Others may be so excited to be away from home on a holiday, that they may not smell a thing. For me, several days a month, I need to figure out how to feel "at home" when clearly I am not back in my bedroom in North Carolina.

Room 803 denotes my temporary address. There is a strange familiarity as I open the door with the bed, desk, chair and sofa all in just about the exact same location as the last room I stayed in. There is not much variance from hotel to hotel. At this point, it's all about the benefits of repeat flying for me! I kind of like the consistencies too, as it helps with getting acclimated faster. (This is particularly helpful at night when I need relief. Tripping over an unanticipated chair or falling is not desired at 2 am.)

Ahh, and there are the anchors to my reality- sitting in linear fashion on the side of the bathroom sink- shampoo, conditioner, and soap. Something I really don't need, but offer more consistency in my environment. Consistency doesn't replace "home," however, it does offer comfort and a sense of stability. It is something I depend on. Have you ever felt weird when one of these three items was missing? For some, it may feel like you have been violated in some way or someone was in your room messing with your stuff. You may call the front desk right away to get the missing items so you can place them in their rightful place on the bathroom sink. Your equilibrium has been restored.

These feelings are not unusual when things we have been accustom to in our environment changes. The analogy of shampoo, conditioner and soap can be applied to familiar anchors in our work life. Our work anchors could be as simple as items on our desk or a location (i.e., office, building, geography). Our reactions are also similar to those described above- we feel violated, unless it was our idea. This chapter will focus on environmental change (in our general work surroundings), since previous chapters discussed other types of organizational change.

CAREER LESSONS LEARNED

- We all need a sense of stability in the workplace. Stability offers the comfort needed for peak performance.
- There is also a need for "healthy" instability to motivate creativity and new ideas, often not found in a stagnant environment.

TIPS FOR USING YOUR SHAMPOO, CONDITIONER AND SOAP

- Identify environmental characteristics that offer you a sense of stability. They are personal in nature. If appropriate, share with your supervisor. Employers cannot assume "one size fits all."

Whether it comes from the boss or elsewhere, all changes to what has become a norm for you are likely to be more effective when you can see the advantages of the proposed change. Even if you cannot change the outcome, knowing early in the process gives you time to adjust.

For example, if you had an office with a window for the last 3 years and your employer moves to a location that takes that away. How does that make you feel? The new desk and chair is a great buffer, but your office is smaller and you had a routine. Several times a week, you would arrive early to work and watered your plants. You enjoyed looking out of the window to see the beautiful maple tree close by, pausing to take a deep breath before charging ahead with work. It was your brief mental check-in to start your day on the right foot. Now all you have is walls and no plants. You feel a sense of loss and as if someone violated your sacred space.

This may sound petty, but it was an important part of your day. Your employer never knew about this routine and never asked. You were told one week ahead of the move to pack. The only information communicated to employees was that the move was financially good for the company.

Your adjustment would have been better received if the communication was earlier, allowing you to figure out another way to gain inner peace at the beginning of your day. Maybe a wall hanging with plants or a mirror to give your office the appearance of more space would have helped. That extra time you used to come in early, could be replaced with a little yoga or a short walk outside with even healthier outcomes.

For Leaders- No environmental change is too small to benefit from inclusion of affected employees in decision-making. The acceptance of the change will be greater and faster. Err on the side of over-communication far in advance of significant environmental change.

There are lots of opportunities for leaders to get employees involved when you know significant environmental changes are in their future.

- Involve your team or co-workers to generate ideas if appropriate.
- Take some time to develop a communication plan which includes timing of roll-out. Address the why, what and how of the change.
- Share progress along the way in staff meetings or 1-1 if there is more of an individual impact than a group impact.
- Never under-estimate the impact small environmental changes can have on productivity and workplace morale. Pay attention to the verbal and non-verbal cues, listen and respond.

Don't over- react to unexpected environmental changes. Having the shampoo, conditioner and soap on the side of the tub may make it easier to reach in the shower. It also may force you to use creative solutions to calm your sense of instability- like buying that strawberry- kiwi shampoo you wanted to try. (At least this might work for the ladies reading this book.)

Stop and think for a moment, when are you the most creative? Is it when things are static or when things are changing- forcing you to do things differently? At first you may resist, but at some point your mind clicks in and you begin to think about all the different scenarios, tactics or tools you will need to adapt to the new variables in front of you. Some may not work, but others may actually take you to a better place than before the change actually occurred.

I remember, as a new CEO at a hospital in Portland, Oregon, I was faced with an office space dilemma for the Administrative Team. They had been previously located in various offices all around the hospital making it difficult to congeal a "team approach" to do our work. I wanted them co-located and our only option was an old ICU that would need to be gutted and reconstructed to allow for one unified Administrative Suite. As you can imagine, the kicking and squealing started immediately, when leaders realized that the environment that they had known, loved and personalized would be radically changed. They would be working side by side with new people and in the same space with the CEO (heaven forbid).

Because I was new, they agreed reluctantly, but I could tell I was really shaking up their world. Privately, I worried that I was making a big mistake as one of the first major things I tackled upon my arrival at this hospital. However, I just knew this would eventually form the foundation for a better team and definitely more efficient work flows.

I gave them as much information along the way as feasible and power in many of the design decisions to increase acceptance. Some were still slow to accept the move, but eventually came around to liking the office flow and their seat buddies. When I stepped down from the position of CEO for this hospital to move on to new things, I still mourn the spirit that lived in that office. To this day, I have yet to experience the interpersonal dynamics of that type of a "high performing team" in any other organization in my career journey. In this case, this environmental instability took the hospital performance to a whole new level!

> *"Start by doing what's necessary; then do what's possible; and suddenly you are doing the impossible"*
>
> **AUTHOR UNKNOWN**

13

Leaving Footprints

"Every perfect traveler always creates the country where he travels."

NIKOS KAZANTZAKIS

"We are what our thoughts have made us; so take care about what you think. Words are secondary. Thoughts live; they travel far."

SWAMI VIVEKANANDA

Every month I touch about six different cities and over twenty organizations. The interactions may be brief, but they are very intense. Early morning meetings, presentations to educate all who will listen, review of critical documents and results, dinner meetings with select executives are all intended to improve performance and the long-term viability of the organizations I coach. As I prepare for my return trip home, I often wonder what they will remember once I am gone. What footprints have I left on these organizations to help them be better for tomorrow? And what footprints have they left on me?

Think about your own travels to different parts of the country, especially places you have never been before. Upon arrival, you quickly begin to take in your surroundings. Your mind acts like a mini-camera, taking pictures that you will draw upon at another time when you reflect on that experience. You meet all kinds of people along the way. Some of them may even make another mental impression that stays with you, good and bad. You may learn new words to add to your vocabulary (sometimes required with foreign travel); cultural nuances unique to the area and you may add a new food to your dietary repertoire. The bottom line is that every new experience changes us in some way, if we are open to it. And, we also leave footprints behind us.

I remember when my husband and I visited Portland, Oregon for the first time when I was interviewing for a job there. We had traveled 3000 miles to get there and discovered immediately one of this country's best kept secrets. Our mental cameras were on overload with the diverse beauty of this place. To add to our mental files, we were overwhelmed with the people- by far the friendliest we had ever met. To this day, both of us can bring up those images with the same vivid descriptions as 14 years ago. Why? Portland, Oregon and its people left footprints in our minds and hearts. Our experiences there changed us. I did end up taking the job and stayed for eight years as the first minority woman ever to run a hospital in the state of Oregon. My husband had become a well- respected youth basketball coach. His boys (now men) call him to this day for continued mentorship. When we decided to move back east, I also knew we had left some footprints in Portland as well.

CAREER LESSONS LEARNED

- It is important to remember that all of us will experience personal change with each organization we work with. The magnitude and characteristics of that change will depend on a variety of variables including our openness to the experience.

- We each have the potential to leave footprints in the workplace. Don't let yours be the ones that vanish in the wind.

Tips to ReciprocalFootprinting

Leave yourself open to really "seeing" the beauty around you. Do you only look for the negative images or positive ones? We sometimes only see what we want to see in both our professional and personal life. Fix your camera lens and try to see it all. Both will be important to your career success.

Have you ever worked with someone who seemed poised to point out the negative in every situation? Their camera lens seemed to be stuck on seeing the glass "half empty." **Negativity narrows your focus and blocks your ability to see much else even if it right in front of you.**

For example,think about when you are stressed out about everything you have to get done in a given day. You may find it hard to actually start anything because you're paralyzed by how long your to-do list has become. Or, if you feel bad about not exercising or not eating healthy, all you think about is how little willpower you have, how you're lazy, and how you don't have any motivation.

In each case, your brain loses sight of any other images and focuses on the negative emotions of fear and anger. Stress adds to your emotional imbalance. Negativity prevents your brain from seeing the other options and choices that surround you.

Conversely, when you are experiencing positive emotions like joy, contentment, and love, you will see more possibilities in your life and broadens your sense of possibilities. Your camera lens is wide open to more options. This doesn't mean you have to always be in a happy dream state either. You need to understand and pay attention to negative or not so acceptable variables around you. The key is that they not consume you or shut your lens to everything else.

Positive thinking isn't just a soft and fluffy feel-good. It's those moments of happiness that are critical for opening your mind to explore and build the skills that become so valuable in career success. Positive and negative outlooks can be very well-ingrained, to the point of seeming instinctive. But they're not. They're habits. And habits can be changed.

Here are some ways you can create a more open camera lens (positive outlook at work):

- Find ways to get in touch with yourself. Mentors can be great mirrors to reflect how you perceive the world. Sometimes an open and honest talk with a mentor can give you a different perspective. Allow yourself to look through someone else's lens. It has often been said that it is never healthy for anyone to just live in their own minds.

- Find appropriate outlets for moments of negativity- meditation, exercise, an outing with friends or a great book can take you to another place mentally and allow you to "see things" in a different way.

- Focus on what is within your control. Staying positive in a difficult work situation requires focusing on those issues that are fully within one's control. It's an internal pursuit, and it starts here: What, specifically, is bothering you? Identifying the issue can help. Staying positive at work is not about ignoring the problems you see; it's about changing the way you see them. However, prolonged negativity can make any "one" issue morph into something bigger than it actually is. The next time you find yourself sinking (deeper) into the negativity hole, take a moment, remove yourself from the situation as much as possible, and take some notes. It will help you sort through the noise and figure out what's actually going on in your head.

Here's a small test. What would your camera lens see?

Situation: Every two years your employer conducts a peer review process to offer employees feedback and personal growth. **Your peer reviews came back 85-percent praise and 15-percent constructive criticism.**

- **Negative:** I got bad reviews this year. I suck at my job.
- **Positive:** Almost everyone thinks I'm good at what I do!

Situation: Several co-workers head out to lunch while you're busy in the copy room.

- **Negative:** They must have waited until I was gone so they wouldn't have to invite me.
- **Positive:** If only I'd finished those copies two minutes earlier! I bet they'll bring me a sandwich if I text right now.

Situation: Your organization just announced a merger with a much larger company.

- **Negative:** I should start shopping now for a new job! This will change us forever.
- **Positive:** I wonder if I will have new professional growth opportunities in a larger organization. This could change us forever.

So, how did you do? Do you have room to adjust your camera lens or does your camera need a complete overhaul?

Consider your organizational legacy. What will people say about you when you leave that organization for another or when you retire? Will your footprints be remembered?

When you woke up this morning to prepare for work, I bet leaving a legacy at work was not at the top of your to do list. For many, just getting through the work day at all is plenty. Legacy is usually attributed to families from royalty, Presidents, or those in significant positions. However, all of us can leave a legacy...contributions that mark our impact on the world, no matter how small. This includes our contributions in the workplace. You don't have to wait until you are ready to leave an organization to start to think about how you will leave it.

Thinking of your job in terms of how you will leave it presents a different way to look at your work and what you want to accomplish. Instead of focusing on day-to-day tasks, it helps you to focus on the bigger picture and take a more global view of your work. Consider your own job, your team, your department, the leadership, and how these pieces are interconnected to make the organization whole. How will you leave your footprint?

Leadership may also benefit from thinking about their work goals and how they may relate to their own legacies. What do they want their employees to be saying about them five or ten years after they depart? Do they want to facilitate growth initiatives or positive organizational change, or develop a program that will change how employees work?

Here are some considerations for creating your organizational legacy:

- **Commit to excellence.** Strive to be your best every day. As you strive for excellence you inspire excellence in others. Excellence can be highly contagious. Serve as a role model for your children, your friends and your colleagues. One person in pursuit of excellence raises the standards and behaviors of everyone around them.

- **Lift others up along the way.** You have a choice. You can lift others up or bring them down. Check your daily workplace interactions. Would you classify yourself as an encourager of others or a discourager? Do you ever think about sharing ideas or best practices with others or hold on to them so only you reap the rewards? Who have you mentored in the last year? Will anyone reach out to you five years from now and say, "Thank you. You made a difference in my life".

- **Be about something greater than yourself. Create a personal mission statement to help define your purpose.** Make your actions count for something. This actually comes full circle to why you choose the job you currently have. If you chose it based on making a difference, you are already on your way to career success and finding joy in your work. Your entire approach to work is grounded in a purpose greater than just a paycheck and can often be a source of energy.

- **Treat others around you with dignity and respect.** My parents would tell me this consideration is about having good "home training" or manners. And, without question, "it's the right thing to do." Listen to my parents!

- **Practice respectful truth-telling.**Constructive feedback to your colleagues and supervisors does not have to be withheld for fear of retribution- most of the time. There will always be that individual, no matter how words are framed, that will lash out against you. (Their camera lens is stuck on the negativity setting.) This is not the norm. If our words are consistently honest and stated in a respectful tone, they will usually be accepted by the receiver, even if they may not want to hear them. Your legacy in this case is "someone others could always count on to tell them the truth"...a respectful attribute.

- **Role model the changes you would like to see in others.** In other words, "walk the talk" and be a leader in small things within your control. Remember you can be a "leader" without holding a title.

So career travelers, check your camera lens, your attitude, your purpose and then check your behavior. Will anyone see your footprints?

Recipe for success;
Be polite, prepare yourself for whatever you
are asked to do, keep yourself tidy,
be cheerful, don't be envious,
be honest with yourself so you will be honest with others,
be helpful, interest yourself in your job, don't pity yourself, be quick to praise,
be loyal to your friends, avoid prejudices,
be independent, interest yourself in politics, and read the newspapers.

BERNARD M. BARUCH, FINANCIER

14

Am I Really Talking to Myself?

"When the traveler goes alone he gets acquainted with himself."
LIBERTY HYDE BAILEY

"The hardest part is to travel, and to be away from your family."
GLENN TIPTON

Finally this trip is coming to an end. I can actually do an early check-in in about an hour for my flight home. It's time to scan the room for all my personal items, pack what I can and co-locate everything else for the morning dash. I catch myself talking out loud as I pace the room. Still talking, I see my reflection in the mirror over the desk. What on earth has happened to me? Who am I talking to? And, when did I go completely over the edge? Did all this alone time finally cause me to crack? I guess its okay as long as I don't hear voices talking back to me.

For a Road Warrior, being alone is standard operating procedure, especially during those hours that are normally spent with family or friends. You eat breakfast alone or not at all and repeat the same ritual once you leave your clients and return to the hotel for respite. Many of us will order room service because we will work through dinner or don't like the feeling of eating alone in the hotel restaurant. As we process our day or things not to forget, one can't help but mumble to ourselves and even talk out loud. I hate to admit, I have even talked back to e-mails that grated my last nerve. I call home and ground myself in a different reality.

Spending this much alone time with yourself is not all bad. Over the last five years on the road, I have experienced a high level of introspection that I may not have explored without it. I have learned a lot about myself and what I desire in my professional and personal life.

CAREER LESSONS LEARNED

- Self-reflection is an important ingredient for career and personal growth and development. It's okay to talk them through out loud- to yourself and others to enhance your perspectives.
- Alone time is not all bad. If used wisely, it can allow you to explore a different part of yourself. The benefits are reaped when you reconnect with others.

TIPS FOR MAXIMIZING YOUR ALONE TIME

Self-Reflection is the way to remove inner road-blocks, to first become aware of the things that are really holding you back and then tackle them by finding a solution. **Keeping a personal journal** is a great way to help you focus. When you read the things you have written, it's the equivalent to listening to yourself talking out loud. Journaling can help you bring personal issues forth from a deeper level of consciousness. You may find yourself more courageous and unfiltered in writing than the spoken word. And, since it is only for you, journaling can help you openand rid yourself of hidden baggage andfree your mind.

Journaling, like talking to yourself, may feel strange at first. Society has conditioned us not to go very deep in dealing with issues...just accept the hand you have been dealt and move on. Yet, moving on without conscious acknowledgement and resolution to the challenges in our life is not healthy. And, the fallout is unexplained emotions or behaviors that pop up in other parts of our life. In the workplace, it can affect our ability to engage in meaningful work, our productivity and ultimately our career success.

Here's how to get started on periodic self-reflection and successful journaling:

- **Find a comfortable place where you can think.** It is helpful to have all of your attention directed to the process. So, turn off the TV and disconnect from your electronics. I like journaling to some quiet music to help me relax. It is best if you don't have anything else on your mind. And, you don't want to get interrupted either. If you are at home with others milling around, go behind a closed door with a sign that reads, "Under Construction-Personal Growth. Come back in an hour."

- **Narrow your search.** Think of your mind like the server for all incoming and outgoing data received daily. When we search our mental files, if the data request is too large, the information we receive back can be too overwhelming to do anything with or too vague. You have to narrow your search with a more discrete data request. In other words, try to pinpoint the key one or two issues you want to reflect upon during this journaling session. This approach will help you stay focused and allow you a deeper exploration of the issues at hand.

- **Think Why? What? How? And Who?** Once you identity the issue, identify why you believe it is important for you to journal about it. What are the barriers you face? How do you proposed to move beyond where you currently stand? Who do you need to share this information with? Who do you need to support your actions for personal growth?

- **Practice respectful truth-telling to yourself!** Being truthful to yourself is the key, without this you won't get very far. Of course, this truth may be unpleasant or even scary. Step out on faith and give it a try. No one is in the room except YOU!

- **Write your best game plan.** You are not looking for perfection here, just your best guess.
- **Make a decision about execution and next steps.** You do not have to act on everything you journal. Sometimes the decision will be that you just needed to vent some emotions privately and that was the barrier you needed to resolve. Other issues may require courageous conversations with family, friends or co-workers. Whatever you choose, don't leave the self-reflection session without making a decision.
- **Share your personal growth with a person you deem as "safe."** This challenge is by choice.

"It is necessary ... for a man to go away by himself ... to sit on a rock ... and ask, 'Who am I, where have I been, and where am I going?'"

Carl Sandburg

"Even if you think you're doing well and have it all figured out, there is a voice you will always inevitably hear at some point which nags at you and says "but wait..." Don't ever dismiss it, listen to what it has to say. Life will never be close enough to perfect, and listening to that voice means stepping outside of yourself and considering your own wrongdoings and flaws."

Ashly Lorenzana

15

My Road Warrior Family

"The things I was allowed to experience, the people I was able to call friends, teammates, mentors, coaches and opponents, the travel, all of it, are far more than anything I ever thought possible in my lifetime."

CURT SCHILLING

Sarah, the Front Desk Manager
Kristy, the Lady Who Brings Me Room Service
Jim, the Taxi Cab Driver in Florida
Fred, the Security Guard at the Raleigh Durham Airport (Why do I know that?)
Lisa, my Client Liaison in Wisconsin
And ...

These are just a few of the members of my Road Warrior family. I know many of their names, especially with clients I have retained for the last five years. I stay at the same hotels to increase my comfort, feel safe, and maintain a moderate sense of consistency in my life on the road. They call me by my formal name when they see me and in an odd way I get the feeling they look out for those who are frequent flyers. It's not unusual for me to have a small treat in my room when I arrive later than they expected, as if they know I am exhausted and haven't eaten much to get to this destination. They smile and act like they really are glad to see me- knowing they are an extension to my "real" family. (Now this could all be my imagination and I am getting great customer service, but I don't care. A Road Warrior will cling on to anything that offers a degree of normalcy, if only in our minds.) These relationships are very important. Minus the consistency work relationships offer in a less mobile job, these kind people have become a part of my work family.

Why do you think there are employers who have an aversion to using the term "family" when defining the workforce and others who openly embrace the concept of a work family? When you think of the definition of family it usual means a unique social group consisting of two parents and children. Some define it as social unit living under one roof with a designated "head" of the household". Sound familiar?

At work, do we not spend 8-10 hours a day under the same roof with our work colleagues with a designated "leader" of the house? For most of us, we spend more waking hours with people at work than we do our own families. Even the relationships we have with our work family mirror our "real family" too! Yes, there will be conflict, but there is also the collegial support needed to facilitate peak performance.

CAREER LESSONS LEARNED

- Work relationships can often mirror the dynamics seen in family structures.
- Positive work relationships are highly correlated with an organization's ability to achieve targeted results.

By nature's design, we are naturally social creatures–we crave friendship and positive interactions, just as we do food and water. So it makes sense that the better our relationships are at work, the happier and more productive we're going to be.

Good working relationships give us several other benefits: our work is more enjoyable when we have good relationships with those around us. Also, people are more likely to go along with changes that we want to implement, and we're more innovative and creative. Another fundamental reason to have positive relationships in the workplace is the direct impact on our paychecks and livelihoods. In order for our job to exist in the future, there is a compelling need to support each other to meet organizational goals and achieve targeted results.

Good relationships are also often necessary if we hope to develop our careers. After all, if your employer doesn't trust you, it's unlikely that he or she will consider you when a new position opens up. Overall, we all want to work with people we're on good terms with.

TIPS TO VALUING YOUR WORK FAMILY

Invest in work relationships.

This *does not* mean you have to cross personal boundaries with people at work. It does mean that you have to value the importance of positive work relationships in facilitating you reaching your career goals. You are not able to advance in a vacuum. Take a co-worker for coffee or take a short walk during breaks. We work better together when we know more about another person than the stories we make up about them in our minds. Foods will always sooth relationships. It's hard to be mad at someone over an ice cream sundae.

Mutually respectful relationships are optimal.

When you respect the people that you work with, you value their input and ideas, and they value yours. Working together, you can develop solutions based on your collective insight, wisdom and creativity.

Be open to others different than yourself.

People with good relationships not only accept diverse people and opinions, but they welcome them. Remember, diversity is bigger than race, culture or ethnicity. Foster a culture of workplace inclusion. Practice active listening to really *hear* what may be important to someone else.

Be aware of how your words and action are received by others.

This means taking responsibility for things you say and how you treat others around you. This includes all kinds of communication- verbal, non-verbal and written. For example, e-mails are always open to interpretation of the reader. Have you ever received an e-mail that shouted at you? How did it make you feel? Clarity of communication is essential to building trusting relationships in the workplace (at home too). Opt for face to face encounters to resolve relationship challenges.

Appreciate another's contributions.

We all like to feel that our hard work is appreciated. Send a thank-you note or just say "well-done". Small acts of kindness go a long way.

Give difficult relationships a chance.

We cannot always work with people we love; however, we should give it our best shot at trying to find a comfortable place to co-exist. Focus more on commonalities and less on differences. If the differences cannot be resolved, get help or ask for an intervention.

> *"Assumptions are the termites of relationships."*
>
> **HENRY WINKLER**

> *"You can talk with someone for years, every day, and still, it won't mean as much as what you can have when you sit in front of someone, not saying a word, yet you feel that person with your heart, you feel like you have known the person for forever.... connections are made with the heart, not the tongue."*
>
> **C. JOYBELL C.**

16

Re-Entry to Your Real Life

"Having to travel so much plays havoc with your personal life."

RENEE FLEMING

"Since I travel so much, it's always great to be home. There's nothing like getting to raid my own refrigerator at two in the morning."

AMY GRANT

As I look out of the plane window, I see the lights and landscape of the place called home. Soon I will hear the wheels come down and the images will appear to grow as touch down becomes imminent. My heart fills with the anticipation of seeing people I love and finally sleeping in my own bed. I have been anticipating this moment all week.

There's the bump of re-entry and we slowly begin to approach the gate. As I collect my things to deplane, other images enter my consciousness-the dance between me and my spouse trying to get used to living under the same roof again. Some may think this is an easy and welcomed adjustment. However, we have lived separate lives for almost a week. All the routine activities of daily living and personal nourishment we share replaced with individual survival tactics until I return. This may sound strange for a couple married for over 36 years, but separation is stressful for all involved. The longer or more consistent the separation, the more difficult re-entry back to your normal life becomes. Separation can precipitate a whole range of emotions, including depression, anger and guilt. On my way to baggage claim, I keep hoping this time will be different.

You don't have to be a Road Warrior to have challenges re-entering your "home life" after a long workday. You may even experience feelings of guilt just preparing to leave for your job in the first place. For working Mom's, these feelings of guilt can be as real as those experienced by the Road Warrior. For the ladies reading this book, see if this scenario sounds familiar (an excerpt from: *The Yellow Suit- A Guide for Women in Leadership*):

> *After a long day at work, you drag your tired mind and body across the threshold to your home, and enter the world where family should be front and center. All day long you have been "talking, talking, talking". The last thing you desire is more talking. If you have children, they are meeting you at the door, anxiously awaiting your attention. You are quietly thinking, somebody...anybody...help me. The whole drive home, all you could think about was a long hot bath, a glass of wine and maybe your husband would be up for a back rub. But as soon as you open the garage, you are snapped back into the reality of dinner, housework, elementary school projects and a husband who demands as much attention as the kids. What made me think I could manage being a leader, working incredible hours and be a good wife and mother? If this describes you...welcome to* female leader guilt.

"Honey, why can't you listen to me," says your husband. "Family is never first for you and what's happening to us? This job is killing our relationship." These sharp statements just compile the guilt you are already feeling.

Then why don't you stop, throw in the career towel and just be the wife and mother everyone wants. Most of the time you want it too (even though you are happy you have a job when the kids are out of control or you have a fight with your husband). You don't throw in the towel because you actually enjoy the role of a leader and all the prestige and recognition that comes with it. And, you worked hard to get there. So guilt takes over as you try and reconcile the challenges of balancing both your desires in your head and heart.

The guilt women feel goes back to a different time in history. A time when there was a societal expectation that women stay home and care of the home, their spouses and children. If they did have a job, there came a time when the woman was expected to leave the job to assume her rightful place at home. Even though that era has passed, the script still plays in our mind. It's what we observed with our parents and it's what we believe our family and friends say behind our back. "She should really be home with those kids and not so wrapped up in that job."

CAREER LESSONS LEARNED

- There will always be tension moving between our work and home lives. Acknowledge the need to address potential stressors with significant others in an attempt to soften your re-entry.
- Cherish quality time with those you love. Try to be "fully present" mind, body and spirit when you are home.

TIPS FOR MANAGING A SUCCESSFUL RE-ENTRY HOME

Make peace with all the reasons you decided to work at this point in your life.

We all work for different reasons. We love our jobs. We need the money. We don't want to risk dropping out of a competitive field when new positions are scarce. We realize we'd be miserable as stay-at-home moms and would make our children unhappy. We want to set an example of a successful, independent wage-earner. We love to lead!

Write down your own motivations. Once you've reassured yourself that you're doing what you need to do, then simply let go of the guilt. Trust yourself and the choices you've made for your family.

Build time to play when you return home.

We all need time to refresh and renew. We actually are better employees when we take the time to breathe and reconnect with our family and friends. Escape with your significant other for an erotic play date, play in the back yard with your children, take a girl trip with your best friend, spend quality time with your parents...allow that other side of you to be free of the daily grind of work, no matter how much you love your job.

If you are a working Mom, acknowledge the loss you may feel leaving your children each day for work.

Remember, no Mom will be able to witness all the wonderful things our children will do and experience in a day. But we can make the times we do share special. There are always tradeoffs for our choices. But, we can make the most of what we do experience with our children. Pay sound attention to balance and teach that to your children as well.

Keep the communication channels open to those who love and support you.

This is often the hardest thing to do, but the most important. Communication and letting out those feeling with a friend or your spouse/partner is an imperative for your mental health. As my husband often tells me, "I can't read your mind. If I knew what you were thinking, maybe I could help. Let me in sometimes. You are not in this alone."

Beware of the "Work Marriage". There's a price to pay for this level of commitment.

It can be tempting to rack up hours at work, especially if you're trying to earn a promotion or manage an ever-increasing workload — or simply keep your head above water. Sometimes overtime might even be required.

If you're spending most of your time working, your home life will take a hit. Some of the consequences can include: fatigue, loss of valuable time with those you love, or maybe more work! You may be able to recover from the fatigue you feel, but the time loss with loved ones is gone forever. With regard to more work, you may be setting a new performance expectation for yourself in the eyes of others. It's like the old commercial that said, "Give it to Mikey, he'll eat anything!"

Remember, managing a healthy re-entry isn't a one-shot deal. Creating work-life balance is a continuous process as your family, interests and work life change. Periodically examine your priorities and make changes if needed.

"I believe that being successful means having a balance of success stories across the many areas of your life. You can't truly be considered successful in your business life if your home life is in shambles".

Zig Ziglar

"What I dream of is an art of balance, of purity and serenity devoid of troubling or depressing subject matter—a soothing, calming influence on the mind, rather like a good armchair which provides relaxation from physical fatigue".

Henri Matisse

17

Here We Go Again!

"You do not travel if you are afraid of the unknown, you travel for the unknown, that reveals you with yourself."

ELLA MAILLAR

"Just to travel is rather boring, but to travel with a purpose is educational and exciting."

SARGENT SHRIVER

Lying on the floor in the spare bedroom is my large yellow suitcase. It almost looks like it's talking to me, with its mouth wide open and flaps to the side waiting to gobble my travel attire for the next trip. This week, California is up next on the schedule. Oh how I hate east coast/west coast plane rides. If the time in the air doesn't kill you, the time zones will. There are moments when I don't know if I am coming or going. These days, it takes about a week after I return home before I feel like my old self again.

Wow, the time back home went by fast. It seems like it was only yesterday when my husband picked me up from the airport...but it's been seven days. That's a long treasured stretch for a Road Warrior. Just when I was starting to remember how it was to have a normal life, **here I go again**.

Some of my friends and family think traveling for work is a glamorous life. These clearly are people who have NEVER been a Road Warrior. Glamour does not describe the lifestyle at all. It is challenging, wears you out physically and may even cause you to talk to yourself. The times alone can be depressing and sometimes scary. And, constant travel can strain the best relationships with significant others.

You may be asking, why do it? Why take on a job that has Road Warrior in the job description? Since I am a glass half-full kind of woman, I know, for me, it was the opportunity to make a difference all over the country. I enjoy and am passionate about facilitating others to be the best they can be. And, stepping out of a straight 9am-5pm job has fulfilled that career desire. After being on the road aggressively for five years, I am getting travel weary and may need to find a different venue to meet that objective. No matter what my next destination in my career journey, I will be taking a suitcase filled with career lessons along with me.

CAREER LESSONS LEARNED

- At each stop in your career journey, fill your suitcase with wisdom and leave some behind for those you encounter along the way.
- Every job contains elements that can prepare you for your next job.

TIPS FOR MOVING TO A NEW CAREER DESTINATION

People change jobs for many reasons — money, boredom, unhappiness, lack of advancement, lack of appreciation, personal conflicts with a supervisor or co-worker, unfair treatment, and many other reasons.

Whenever you consider moving to a new job, ask yourself a series of questions.

- Am I still enjoying my current job? Am I still growing professionally or standing still?
- Am I leaving for something better?
- Have I done all the homework I need to do on the new organization to make a good decision?
- Will I be compensated fairly for my professional worth?
- Are emotions driving my decision to leave?
- Will this be a better fit for me and my family at this time in my career journey?

No matter what the reason is for changing jobs, the decision should be a *rational* decision—not an emotional one. And money alone, unless it's a great deal of money, shouldn't be the sole factor for leaving a job.

If you do decide to make a change, you might first want to look at job opportunities within your current company. Sometimes it's easier to make a lateral move inside the company than to leave the company altogether. Some companies actually prefer hiring workers they know from within rather than gambling on outside applicants they don't know.

If you like what you do but don't like where you work, you probably should consider a job change. If you don't like what you do, you should be looking at a career change.

Career changes, unless you're very young, are usually the hardest to make. Often career changes require new training or education, and a willingness to return to an entry-level position when you're hired by a company in the new career field. If you're young, it's usually much easier to do. But the older you are, the harder it is to accomplish, and the more you have to sacrifice, especially financially.

Analyze your feelings. Trust your instincts. If what you're doing doesn't feel right, make a change. It's much easier to succeed and move ahead in a field where you feel you really belong. And in a field you really enjoy.

"People who are unable to motivate themselves must be content with mediocrity, no matter how impressive their other talents."

Andrew Carnegie

"Believe in yourself! Have faith in your abilities! Without a humble but reasonable confidence in your own powers you cannot be successful or happy."

Norman Vincent Peale

18

Destination Infinity (final thoughts)

*"If you want to succeed you should strike out on new paths,
rather than travel the worn paths of accepted success."*

JOHN D. ROCKEFELLER

*"It is for us to pray not for tasks equal to our powers, but for pow-
ers equal to our tasks, to go forward with a great desire forever beat-
ing at the door of our hearts as we travel toward our distant goal."*

HELEN KELLER

By now you probably have figured out that this book is not about travel. If you have been taking in all the sights along the way, you hopefully realized this is a travel guide to a successful career. Where you go and
how far you travel is all up to you.

Each chapter contained important elements to add to your personal luggage. For those of you further along in your career, your luggage may exceed the weight limit- filled with all the wisdom collected on your journey. For early careerists, it may feel light for now. The goal is not to empty your luggage but continue to add to its contents. In other words, strive to be continuous learners. And, if you do choose to lighten your load, pass on what you have learned to another career traveler. Be like the little boy in the movie and *"Pay It Forward."*

Sometimes, we limit the depth of our journey by putting timelines and "titles" around each stop along the way. These well-constructed five-year career plans can sometimes block your ability to see other opportunities right in front of you that may have taken you to a destination you never thought possible. It's okay to look at the possibilities available to you and choose the path where your journey will begin.

We select the schools we think will position us for the future, we scan multiple job listings for a possible match and, we listen to family, friends and colleagues for what should be our best choice. We even think about how much money we want to make. After that, we plow ahead and get on the bus, plane or train to that destination. Once we board and in motion to that destination, everything else passes quickly outside the window- becoming white background noise. We essentially close our minds to other possibilities.

I once had a student ask me, "Mrs. Gaines, how long did it take you to learn all this stuff?" He was a health management intern at the hospital where I was the CEO. He had a detailed three-year plan (not five) and was determined to make a six-figure salary by the end of the three years. When I told him over 30 years, I thought the poor young man would faint. He continued, "I cannot wait 30 years to be you. Please tell me the fast track methodology to becoming a CEO."

Wow, there was no sight- seeing for this young man. And, he definitely would be traveling light. With limited **"on the job"** skills and limited wisdom in his luggage- his itinerary would be very short at each destination. His educational prep was great, but in today's world it only gets you so far.

Traveling all over the United States for the last five years, I have witnessed the fallout of the **"light luggage syndrome."** Today, there are lots of fresh young faces graduating from all types of colleges and universities with an alphabet soup of degrees. MBA's, MHA's and more are believed to be an instant passport to the C- Suite. What happen to the good old days of paying your dues to before advancement? It may not take 30 years to get there, but the knowledge, skills and wisdom to be a Chief Executive or any top leadership job is not achieved solely with a master's degree. There is still something to be said for stopping along your career journey and taking in the sights from a more experienced traveler. It's even better if you seek out a mentor as a guide. (Think about it...a mountain climber has enough sense to take a Sherpa along for the journey to a mountain's peak. They know stuff that will help them achieve their goals!)

I am convinced, the **"light luggage syndrome"**sets up organizations and the people they hire who are traveling light, for failure. Nothing replaces the lessons learned when you assimilate what you have learned in theory with the real work world. I have certainly learned from my successes (some trial and error in the early days) and my failures. Maybe more from my failures because I know what I never want to repeat. The various mentors in my life helped me to see all the sights I was missing. They opened my eyes to new destinations to explore.

For instance, I started my career as a registered nurse. If someone had told me I would one day be a Regional Chief Executive for a Health System, a National Speaker and Best-Selling Author, I would have told them they were lying or had lost their mind. I did not come to these new destinations with a five-year career plan in hand. Multiple stops in multiple cities with both eyes and heart wide open allowed me to fill my luggage with essential souvenirs needed to get me to my current career location. Some days, when I reflect back, pulling out all the photos in my mental scrapbook, I still can't believe it.

So, throw away that old five-year plan and follow your passion. It may be blocking your ability to **see** other things. What type of work really brings you joy and makes you feel like you are making a meaningful contribution? Keep both eyes open to all the world has to offer. Listen to the many voices (including complete strangers)that may have wisdom to inform your career travel plans.

Destination Infinity means the there is no limit to your career possibilities unless <u>you</u> place it there.

Until our next journey,

Jackie

"My message, especially to young people is to have courage to think differently, courage to invent, to travel the unexplored path, courage to discover the impossible and to conquer the problems and succeed. These are great qualities that they must work towards. This is my message to the young people."

ABDUL KALAM

19

My Career Travel Journal

Using the career lessons learned throughout the book, assess your own strengths and opportunities for growth and professional development. Create an *action plan* to move you closer to your destination. And remember, there is no end to where you land or what you can achieve-destination infinity!

FOUR KEY SUCCESS FACTORS TO CONSIDER AS YOU FACE A NEW WORK DAY:

- Advanced preparation
- Attention to work-life balance
- Adding value to your chosen profession
- Interactions that are genuine in words and actions

Action Plan

Packing what you need for a successful journey

Be deliberate in researching organizational and cultural norms of the places you would like to work- before hire.

Don't leave your common sense and intuition at home when interviewing. It's better to over-analyze cultural fit rather than make a bad decision affecting your future.

After hire, stay alert to shifts in culture. If the compromise required for alignment to the new culture will dramatically affect your personal integrity or well-being...start shopping for a new job.

Action Plan

SURVIVING THE ORGANIZATIONAL PAT DOWN

All work will require ongoing mental and emotional readjustments every day. Your ability to comply is directly influenced by the magnitude of the readjustment, past experiences, rewards and recognition and the perceived risk of "non-compliance".

Know the organizational "rules." This includes standards of behavior or codes of conduct- written and unwritten. Knowledge is a powerful antidote for the unknown and fear-based emotions.

Action Plan

_____

_____

_____

_____

_____

_____

CLARITY OF VISION

Be aware of first impressions –they directly impact relationships and decision-making in the workplace.

Validate your assumptions...better yet, ask before you assume.

Action Plan

_____

_____

_____

_____

_____

_____

_____

MITIGATING THE POTENTIAL RISKS OF TRAVEL

During our career lifetime, we all will face times when the choices ahead of us seem less than optimal. Weigh the risk and the benefit of each choice, then move forward. Put more personal energy appreciating the benefits of that choice than dwelling on the lack of a perfect fit...at least until you are able to find a more optimal choice.

If you always wait for the perfect choice, you may deprive yourself of needed essentials.

Mitigate the risks if possible.

Action Plan

_____

_____

_____

_____

_____

_____

Managing a change in travel plans

Best laid plans are subject to change. In fact, all we can count on in any job is that *change* will be a constant. How you respond to change *is* within your power to control.

Find the "pearl" in your oyster. In other words, what good can come out of situations beyond your control? (I don't like oysters, so this analogy worked for me.) My pearl in this horrific travel experience- my mini workout.

Action Plan

_____

_____

_____

_____

_____

_____

Surviving and undesirable seat buddy

We cannot choose our coworkers, but we can choose how we interact with them.

Elevate commonalities

Explore differences

Respectfully confront tensions to enhance workplace relationships

Leadership has the opportunity to take multiple variables into consideration to align employees with corporate culture upon hire.

Action Plan

_____

_____

_____

_____

_____

_____

Appreciating the beauty of clouds

Everyone needs time throughout the work week to pause, think and breathe.

Constant "doing" may only yield exhaustion and not results. Quality work is not found when one is in constant motion.

The investment in a "time to plan" or "re-evaluate actions to date" may actually yield better results and time left over to exhale.

Action Plan

_____

_____

_____

_____

_____

_____

Surviving organizational turbulence

Change or fear of the unknown can cause people to feel insecure about their jobs. They aren't quite sure what's going to happen with the organization. As a result, they might gossip, speculating or spreading false rumors. This is human nature's way of coping; people are trying to understand and gather information so they feel safe.

Not all employees will respond to the unknown in the same way. They may share the initial shock of something new (anticipated turbulence); however, some may embrace changes to come.

Leaders should always err on the side of over-communication, especially as it relates to any organizational turbulence.

Action Plan

_____

_____

_____

_____

_____

_____

Acclimating to a whole new culture

Cultural resets are reoccurring requirements in the workplace.

Choose cultural fit wisely before accepting a new job. Prevention is better than a forced acceptance once hired.

Think broader than race or ethnicity when thinking of culture. Cultural resets will include acclimating to a variety of people different than ourselves, organizational dynamics and new environments.

Cultural resets do not require you to lose your own identity, just to be open to something new with respectful engagement.

Action Plan

_____

_____

_____

_____

_____

_____

USING THE ORGANIZATIONAL GPS

All organizations need a GPS to reach their strategic goals and sustain viability for the future.

An organizational GPS offers employees turn by turn instructions on how to execute on specific goals. They must be thoughtful, communicated with clarity and flexible enough to allow for course corrections throughout the organization's journey. Leadership must periodically pause to check for accuracy of data loaded into the GPS and update as needed.

Once employees understand the organization's road map, compliance with the turn by turn instructions become a matter of skill or will. Do you have the skill to complete the task? Do you want to complete the task (will)? There is a price to pay for non-compliance. Think of it as your "toll".

Action Plan

_____

_____

_____

_____

_____

_____

USING YOUR SHAMPOO, CONDITIONER AND SOAP

We all need a sense of stability in the workplace. Stability offers the comfort needed for peak performance.

There is also a need for "healthy" instability to motivate creativity and new ideas, often not found in a stagnant environment.

Action Plan

_____

_____

_____

_____

_____

_____

LEAVING FOOTPRINTS

It is important to remember that all of us will experience personal change with each organization we work with. The magnitude and characteristics of that change will depend on a variety of variables including our openness to the experience.

We each have the potential to leave footprints in the workplace. Don't let yours be the ones that vanish in the wind.

Action Plan

_____

_____

_____

_____

_____

Maximizing your alone time

Self-reflection is an important ingredient for career and personal growth and development. It's okay to talk them through *out loud-* to yourself and others to enhance your perspectives.

Alone time is not all bad. If used wisely, it can allow you to explore a different part of yourself. The benefits are reaped when you reconnect with others.

Action Plan

_____

_____

_____

_____

_____

VALUING YOUR WORK FAMILY

Work relationships can often mirror the dynamics seen in family structures.

Positive work relationships are highly correlated with an organization's ability to achieve targeted results.

Action Plan

_____

_____

_____

_____

_____

_____

_____

MANAGING A SUCCESSFUL RE-ENTRY "HOME".

There will always be tension moving between our *work* and *home* lives. Acknowledge the need to address potential stressors with significant others in an attempt to soften your re-entry.

Cherish quality time with those you love. Try to be "fully present" mind, body and spirit when you are home.

Action Plan

_____

_____

_____

_____

_____

_____

_____

MOVING TO A NEW CAREER DESTINATION

At each stop in your career journey, fill your suitcase with wisdom and leave some behind for those you encounter along the way.

Every job contains elements that can prepare you for your next job.

Action Plan

_____

_____

_____

_____

_____

_____

GET YOUR PASSPORT STAMPED TO DESTINATION INFINITY

Remember, talking about your career aspirations, as well as challenges to another person expedites your trip. Challenge yourself to take one or two items from your career journal and discuss with your boss or mentor over the next 60 days. You are on your way!

Career Action Plan:

_____

_____

_____

_____

_____

Date Shared:

_____

_____

_____

_____

Reviewed/Supported By:

_____

_____

_____

_____

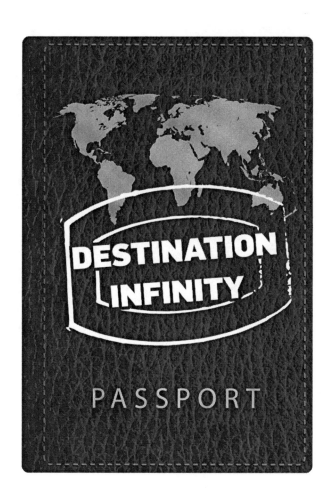

ABOUT THE AUTHOR

Jackie is a high performing Senior Executive with a progressive career encompassing more than 30 years of sustained leadership and accomplishments with major health systems and organizations. With passion, creative energy and vision, she motivates diverse groups of people toward success. She has dedicated most of her career to the advancement of quality health care programs throughout the United States, particularly those focused on the care of the poor and underserved. She has worked in a variety of roles, starting her career as a nurse working for Johns Hopkins Health Institutions, including management, health education, and program coordination. Upon graduation from her master's program she went to work for Health Care for the Homeless, Inc. in Baltimore, Maryland as a Nurse Practitioner serving over 50,000 vulnerable patients per year in clinics, shelters and the streets. In 1987, she was appointed as its first President & CEO and developed this organization into a national model.

In 1999, Jackie was appointed Vice President of Community Health Systems Integration for Bon Secours Baltimore Health System. There

Jackie led an effective $15 million turn-around initiative called Transformation 2000. In 2000 Jackie joined the Providence Health System in Oregon, as Chief Executive for Providence Milwaukee Hospital and Regional Chief Executive for Ancillary Business. While at Providence, Jackie took Providence Milwaukee to Top 100 Hospital in the U.S. three times and implemented the organization's Family Practice Residency Program. In 2007 Jackie left Providence to become the President and CEO of Mercy Health Partners for Northeast Pennsylvania, where she had oversight for two hospitals and 15 other freestanding clinics and diagnostic centers.

Jackie lectures all over the country and has received numerous awards along the way. She has written and published two best-selling books. "Believing You Can Fly"offers insight to her career journey in an attempt to inspire others to pursue their dreams against what may seem to be insurmountable odds. And, "The Yellow Suit- A Guide for Women in Leadership" offers women a simple guide rich with tips on how to be a highly effective leader in today's world, despite the fact that the scales of equality are not quite balanced in the workplace.

Today, Jackie is an Executive Leadership Coach and National Speaker for Studer Group. She lives in North Carolina with her husband Wesley, enjoying the beauty and rich culture of the area.

Here's a sneak peek into Jacquelyn Gaines's best sellers.
Receiving 5-Star reviews on Amazon.com!

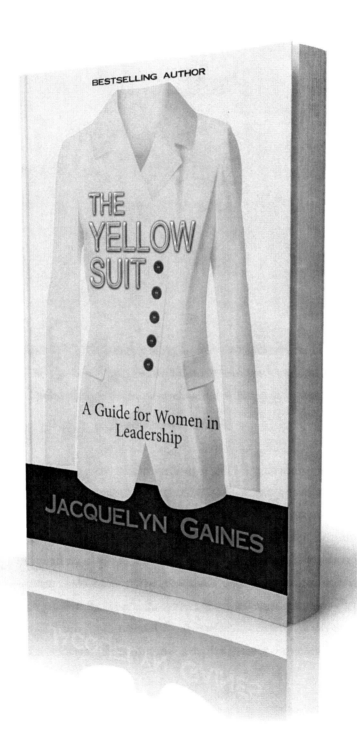

PRELUDE

"We all should know that diversity makes for a rich tapestry, and we must understand that all the threads of the tapestry are equal in value no matter what their color."

MAYA ANGELOU

I remember preparing for the interview like it was yesterday. I pulled out every suit in my closet ...black, navy blue, brown tweed, another black one and then my array of beautiful tailored colored suits, pink, baby blue and a muted yellow that I adored. Colors made me feel alive and I am very comfortable with being a woman. The voice in my head from my *Dress for Success* class screamed at me, "black suit, white shirt, black pumps and light jewelry"–the corporate uniform expected of anyone striving to experience the upper stratosphere of leadership. When on earth did this mandate begin? I can guarantee it wasn't from a woman. And, probably came from an era when woman first crossed the boundaries into leadership roles primarily held by men. Blending into the leadership culture meant relinquishing femininity for a masculine look and feel equated with power. Even to this day, it continues to be taught at universities all over the country as the preferred interview ensemble as our leaders for tomorrow prepare to enter the workforce, perpetuating the gender bias in corporate America.

On this day, I was preparing for an interview that would advance my career to the next level of leadership, the Chief Executive of a hospital. This was a job held by few women across the country and one I never thought I would be offered in my lifetime. First impressions would be critical for both parties- me as the candidate and for them as the employer. Being the first woman hired to this leadership team meant I had to fit their culture. Moving my family 3000 miles for this job meant this better be a good fit for me as well. As I scanned my options of what to wear, all I could think about was the power of first impressions and the most important element when considering such a huge decision that would impact me professionally and personally. I needed to present as a credible professional and be true to myself. If they want you as their leader, it's not about the color of your suit...but the color of your character and your abilities. So, I went with the yellow suit.

I could stop the story here, but it gets better. On the day of the interview I happen to cross paths with the two other candidates competing for this job. One was a man and one was a woman. It should be no surprise that both wore blue suits, white shirts and black shoes. Oh yeah, the man wore a red tie (surprised?). As the day progressed, the interviews went quite well. I enjoyed the dialogue. There was laughter and a great exchange. I got a good sense of them and I believe they got a good sense of me. Once I returned back to my hotel, I got a call from the recruiter who confirmed what I felt, I was a hit! The recruiter went on to say, "The yellow suit took you over the top. The report back to the CEO was that any woman who feels that comfortable with herself to wear a yellow suit to an interview is the kind of leader we want for our hospital." The next day I was offered the job and broke all the *Dress for Success* rules.

Breaking this long standing gender biased dress code will be difficult because women contribute to the madness. We must learn to be comfortable with who we are and not to buy into the belief that women must assume the characteristics of men in order to be effective leaders. In fact, women have innate and learned characteristics that can serve well in today's business environment. **It's time to build a new paradigm that uses the best of both sexes as a determinant of what makes a successful leader.** And the male dominant world of business will need to listen.

This book will explore the role of gender in leadership and the unique ingredients women add to the achievement of successful outcomes in business. Many of the stories are based on my own experiences as a woman leader in the health care industry for over 30 years and shared by thousands of women throughout the country.

Women should feel proud of the attributes they bring to any organization. Our touch is unique and doesn't have to be masked or perceived as a sign of weakness. We just need to believe in our own inner strength. We are effective leaders being fully who we are...leading our way.

WHAT PEOPLE ARE SAYING ABOUT THE YELLOW SUIT- A GUIDE FOR WOMEN IN LEADERSHIP...

The Yellow Suit: A Guide for Women in Leadership book is a true inspirational testament anyone already in or interested in a leadership role. Jackie Gaines is an incredible writer and helps to break the barriers in achieving leadership. She makes it real for those of us who face these day to day challenges. I am grateful for this wonderful book and the inspiration it has given me. I would highly recommend this book to anyone who has faced their own challenges in the working world; it is well worth the read!!

LISA SCHLACK—Global Program Manager, Cisco Systems

What an awesome book! I have read many books that dealt with women in leadership and never found one that was more motivating and inspiring than The Yellow Suit book!!! This book is a must for all women that is in a leadership role or have the desire to be in a leadership role! I have learned from this book how to handle many situations on my job! Thank you so much for bringing the world an outstanding leadership book for women!!!

TANYA WRIGHT—Retail Account Executive, Parlux

I really love this book! I recommend this book to the countless women who aspire to be the best they can be in their careers. I have read this book again and again. It has truly changed my life! It has taught me valuable lessons that I use in my day to day operation! Thanks, Jacquelyn for writing this wonderful, much-needed book! God Bless you!

ALICIA PERRY—President and CEO of Arrie Publishing Company

What a wonderful and much needed book. I loved the way she designed the book so that readers can chose chapters to fit their current needs. This is such an excellent book for women entering their first leadership position. I especially enjoyed her use of stories and her choice of inspirational quotes.

Jacquelyn writes in a way that captures your attention and allows the reader to become the leader she describes. Having met this author and worked with her, I see her as a wonderful role model, teacher, and an inspiration to everyone. She has given the reader the ability to recognize their internal power, and a framework to make the most of themselves and their careers. This is a very good book to give as a graduation gift for future leaders."

CATHY GRUBBS—Coach Specialist, The Studer Group

This inspiring book shares one woman's experiences in the health care field, as she overcame prejudice to excel in her career

This is the true story of a woman who turned her dream of helping people into a rewarding thirty-year career in health care.

Jacquelyn Gaines joined the workforce as a nurse. Her dedication and compassion made her a favorite among her patients, but her superiors weren't always so impressed. As a black woman, she faced their prejudices and proved her worth.

Eventually deciding to take her career to another level, her professional and personal life were forever changed when she started working for Health Care for the Homeless, Inc., in Baltimore, Maryland. Again her empathy, paired with hard work, made her interactions with her patients fruitful and fulfilling.

"I have never worked anywhere before or since that gave me such a sense of purpose," she writes. "I knew daily that I made a difference in the lives of the vulnerable people in the community where I was born and raised."

She later took on the position of Vice President of Community Health Systems Integration for Bon Secours Baltimore Health System and worked with the Surgeon General. Then, at the top of her career, she became the first black female to run a hospital in Oregon and later served as the Regional President and CEO for Mercy Health Partners in Northeast Pennsylvania.

Gaines now shares her experiences to motivate and inspire those with similar aspirations.

Thank You From The Publisher

Thank you for reading an Arrie Publishing Company book. We hope you enjoyed this book, and we encourage you to share your thoughts with us or write a review. This book is available in Paperback, e-Book and Audio.

Please visit our website at www.arriepublishingcompany.com to find more of Jacquelyn Gaines's books.

CPSIA information can be obtained at www.ICGtesting.com
Printed in the USA
BVOW05s0203130214

344828BV00005B/20/P